I0890788

Legal, Safety, and Environmental Challenges for Event Management:

Emerging Research and Opportunities

Vipin Nadda
University of Sunderland, London, UK

Ian Arnott
University of Westminster, London, UK

Wendy Sealy
University of Chichester, UK

A volume in the Advances in Logistics, Operations, and Management Science (ALOMS) Book Series

IGI Global
DISSEMINATOR OF KNOWLEDGE

Published in the United States of America by
IGI Global
Business Science Reference (an imprint of IGI Global)
701 E. Chocolate Avenue
Hershey PA, USA 17033
Tel: 717-533-8845
Fax: 717-533-8661
E-mail: cust@igi-global.com
Web site: http://www.igi-global.com

Library of Congress Cataloging-in-Publication Data

Names: Nadda, Vipin, 1970- editor. | Arnott, Ian, 1970- editor. | Sealy, Wendy, 1961- editor.
Title: Legal, safety, and environmental challenges for event management : emerging research and opportunities / Vipin Nadda, Ian Arnott, and Wendy Sealy, editors.
Description: Hershey, PA : Business Science Reference, 2020. | Includes bibliographical references and index. | Summary: "This book examines the various dimensions of organizing and managing events that include risk management, legal issues, risk assessment, and the environmental impact of events"-- Provided by publisher.
Identifiers: LCCN 2019049669 (print) | LCCN 2019049670 (ebook) | ISBN 9781799832300 (hardcover) | ISBN 9781799832317 (paperback) | ISBN 9781799832324 (ebook)
Subjects: LCSH: Special events--Management. | Special events--Safety measures. | Risk management.
Classification: LCC GT3405 .L45 2020 (print) | LCC GT3405 (ebook) | DDC 394.2--dc23
LC record available at https://lccn.loc.gov/2019049669
LC ebook record available at https://lccn.loc.gov/2019049670

This book is published in the IGI Global book series Advances in Logistics, Operations, and Management Science (ALOMS) (ISSN: 2327-350X; eISSN: 2327-3518)

British Cataloguing in Publication Data
A Cataloguing in Publication record for this book is available from the British Library.

All work contributed to this book is new, previously-unpublished material.
The views expressed in this book are those of the authors, but not necessarily of the publisher.

For electronic access to this publication, please contact: eresources@igi-global.com.

Advances in Logistics, Operations, and Management Science (ALOMS) Book Series

ISSN:2327-350X
EISSN:2327-3518

Editor-in-Chief: *John Wang* Montclair State University, USA

MISSION

Operations research and management science continue to influence business processes, administration, and management information systems, particularly in covering the application methods for decision-making processes. New case studies and applications on management science, operations management, social sciences, and other behavioral sciences have been incorporated into business and organizations real-world objectives.

The **Advances in Logistics, Operations, and Management Science** (ALOMS) Book Series provides a collection of reference publications on the current trends, applications, theories, and practices in the management science field. Providing relevant and current research, this series and its individual publications would be useful for academics, researchers, scholars, and practitioners interested in improving decision making models and business functions.

COVERAGE

- Information Management
- Production Management
- Risk Management
- Finance
- Political Science
- Networks
- Decision analysis and decision support
- Marketing engineering
- Operations Management
- Services management

IGI Global is currently accepting manuscripts for publication within this series. To submit a proposal for a volume in this series, please contact our Acquisition Editors at Acquisitions@igi-global.com or visit: http://www.igi-global.com/publish/.

The Advances in Logistics, Operations, and Management Science (ALOMS) Book Series (ISSN 2327-350X) is published by IGI Global, 701 E. Chocolate Avenue, Hershey, PA 17033-1240, USA, www.igi-global.com. This series is composed of titles available for purchase individually; each title is edited to be contextually exclusive from any other title within the series. For pricing and ordering information please visit http://www.igi-global.com/book-series/advances-logistics-operations-management-science/37170. Postmaster: Send all address changes to above address.

Titles in this Series

For a list of additional titles in this series, please visit:
http://www.igi-global.com/book-series/advances-logistics-operations-management-science/37170

Multi-Criteria Decision Analysis in Management
Abhishek Behl (Indian Institute of Technology, Bombay, India)
Business Science Reference • © 2020 • 422pp • H/C (ISBN: 9781799822165) • US $245.00

Handbook of Research on Project Management Strategies and Tools for Organizational Success
Nelson Antonio Moreno-Monsalve (Universidad EAN, Colombia) H. Mauricio Diez-Silva (Universidad EAN, Colombia) Flor Nancy Diaz-Piraquive (Universidad Catolica de Colombia, Colombia) and Rafael Ignacio Perez-Uribe (Universidad EAN, Colombia)
Business Science Reference • © 2020 • 537pp • H/C (ISBN: 9781799819349) • US $285.00

Advancing Skill Development for Business Managers in Industry 4.0 Emerging Research and Opportunities
Sara Fazzin (H-Farm College, UK)
Business Science Reference • © 2020 • 168pp • H/C (ISBN: 9781799820369) • US $185.00

Management and Inter/Intra Organizational Relationships in the Textile and Apparel Industry
Vasilica-Maria Margalina (Technical University of Ambato, Ecuador) and José M. Lavín (CESINE University Centre, Spain)
Business Science Reference • © 2020 • 427pp • H/C (ISBN: 9781799818595) • US $215.00

Neutrosophic Sets in Decision Analysis and Operations Research
Mohamed Abdel-Basset (Zagazig University, Egypt) and Florentin Smarandache (University of New Mexico, USA)
Engineering Science Reference • © 2020 • 300pp • H/C (ISBN: 9781799825555) • US $245.00

For an entire list of titles in this series, please visit:
http://www.igi-global.com/book-series/advances-logistics-operations-management-science/37170

IGI Global
DISSEMINATOR OF KNOWLEDGE

701 East Chocolate Avenue, Hershey, PA 17033, USA
Tel: 717-533-8845 x100 • Fax: 717-533-8661
E-Mail: cust@igi-global.com • www.igi-global.com

Table of Contents

Preface

Events industry today is developing at a very fast pace throughout the world. Organising and managing events is a massive task and need professional acumen. However, if done meticulously, can enhance the sustainability and competitiveness of both, destination as well as business organisation.

An event is composed of a set of activities with specific purpose goals and needs of the attendees. Today event managers can choose from a wide range of venues and open spaces to host their events. Risk Management is a key requirement of these 'organized occasions'. Since the 1980s, employers in the UK have been subject to statutory responsibilities to ensure that all workplaces are safe. These responsibilities also extend to event managers staging events. The Corporate Manslaughter Act of 1997 and the Health and Safety Act 1999 have invariably changed the way that events are planned, managed and delivered.

This book is an effort to provide an insight of legal, health& safety risks and environmental challenges for events management.

In terms of the structure of this book:

Chapter 1 highlights useful models such the EMBOK and also the five step process to enable both practitioners and those wishing to gain a greater knowledge and understanding on what can potentially be a complex area. This is further supported with a body of knowledge of those who have written in the area and support some the ideas that have been presented

Chapter 2 highlights Health and safety management is organized efforts and procedures for identifying workplace hazards risk and reducing accidents and exposure to harmful situations and substances. It also includes a system of organisational culture, climate, process, procedures, policies, strategies and training of personnel in accident prevention, accident response, emergency preparedness, and use of protective clothing and equipment. An event organiser have a duty of care – to both your attendees and your staff. The larger is an event, more important will be the need for managing health and safety risks.

Chapter 3 highlights the sustainability and development related to corporate social responsibility is assessed throughout the meetings. The intermediate approaches of group thinking and its future possibilities are discussed in brief. It will be helpful to break the orthodox mentality and also for future purpose to bring development and innovation in the society. The techniques of current approaches regarding the thinking process and their impact on the society is assessed. The group thinking has been assessed through a particular mentality of the group in the different society in the country. The process of implementing change in the recent mentality and the platform to implement the process has been analyzed in the context of learning and development.

Chapter 4 examines best practices for managing major health and safety issues at outdoor music festivals (OMFs) based on an extensive literature review and the author's practitioner experience of various music festivals nationwide. It will provide a practical and convenient reference guide for event managers who do not have time to attend other training or to do extensive research. The chapter is organised into sections. The first section will discuss the legislative framework for outdoor events in the UK. Next, commentary is provided on the nature and characteristics of outdoor music festivals. Common risks associated with outdoor music festivals are discussed accompanied by actionable steps that event managers can employ to mitigate risks. The chapter will assist event managers in operationalizing their event safety plans for outdoor music festivals.

Chapter 5 provides advice on how to prepare to negotiate with a venue through an exploration of contract terminology, hire charges and the principles of yield management. Once signed, the contract is a legally binding document that will govern how the event will be run and this chapter will also provide an overview of licencing and health and safety guidance and demonstrates how this is embedded in venue contracts.

Chapter 6 explores theoretically the difficult interrelation between terrorism and event management as well as the conceptual limitations of western rationality to understand the 'undesired Other'.

Chapter 7 provides a useful insight to some of the areas that need to be considered in the practise of Health and Safety being underpinned by recent research and legislation within the world of Events Management. It is also underpinned with guidance of some of the frameworks that can help.

Vipin Nadda
University of Sunderland, London, UK

Chapter 1
Risk Managment in Events Management

Ian Arnott
University of Sunderland, London, UK

ABSTRACT

Risk management is a key requirement in the events industry today. All elements in event delivery have to be considered in the decision to deliver the event during the planning phase, and this information has to be shared with all the stakeholders so that they are able to input it to the document. The chapter highlights useful models such the EMBOK and also the five-step process to enable both practitioners and those wishing to gain a greater knowledge and understanding on what can potentially be a complex area. This is further supported with a body of knowledge of those who have written in the area and support some the ideas that have been presented.

INTRODUCTION

There have been many working definitions put forward for risk management, in particular in the field of event. Bowdin, Allen, OToole, Harris and Mcdonnell (2008) suggested that any event risk is the future incident that will negatively influence the event. Whereas Ritchie and Reid (2017) more recent definition put forward the view that events have the potential to generate internal and external risks and crises, due to their size, scope, use of equipment, and attraction of large numbers of people to particular site (s) during a defined period therefore any potential risks need to be considered. Those these are useful to consider what it is clearly evident from this that due to size and diversity of the events industry which was highlighted Bowdin et al (2008) that risk management must form an essential part of an event manager's

DOI: 10.4018/978-1-7998-3230-0.ch001

practice. Getz (2002) reveals that festival crises event failures are common; he identified the primary reason for event failure as the lack of advanced or strategic planning. This could also be down to that event organisers lack some of the knowledge in this area or the foresight in its planning. Wat must be noted from this that risk management assists event organisers in devising and conducting events in the safest possible manner, while mitigating losses and setting standards (Berloghi, 1994).

The British Standards Institution (BSI, 2002) defines risk management as the: *Systematic application of management policies, procedures and practices to the tasks of establishing the context, analysing, evaluating, treating, monitoring and communicating risk.*

What is clearly evident from this definition is that event managers/have a legal and ethical responsibility, health and safety, loss prevention, emergency preparedness, and need to make good decision making (Rutherford -Silvers, 2008) towards the management of this area and its planning.

The panning process begins with the identification of possible threats and hazards in various risks 'fields' such as finance, health or the environment (Getz and Page, 2016). This is can accompany 'task analyses in project planning, as recommended by O'Toole and Mikolatis (2002). Next, an assessment of risk probabilities' (how likely they are to occur) and severity (how serious are the consequences) leads to a matrix analysis of probability times severity (Getz and Page, 2016). Silvers (2008) also integrates the risk assessment process with the various elements of EMBOK (Event Management Body of Knowledge) (see Figure 1)

Figure 1. Event Management Body of Knowledge (EMBOK)

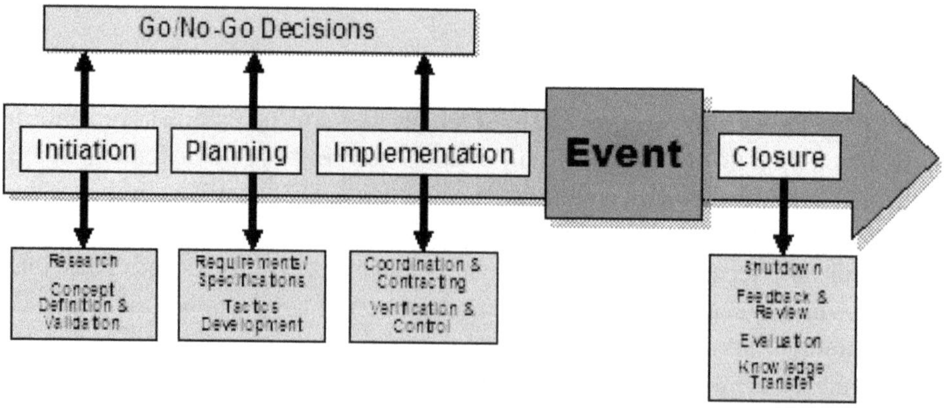

Though we have established that risk management is an essential part of the events industry event managers need to understand what each word is in order to establish, or help them apply the appropriate health, safety and risk management plans.

They can be defined as Bladen, Kennel, Abson and Wilder (2012) put forward.

- **Hazard:** Anything which has the potential to cause harm to people. This could be a dangerous property of an item or a substance, a condition, a situation or an activity.
- **Risk:** The likelihood that the harm from a hazard is realised and the extent of it. In a risk assessment, risk should reflect both the likelihood that harm will occur and the severity of it.
- **Risk Assessment:** The formal assessment of the relevant hazards and the potential severity of the outcome.
- **Risk Control:** Methods employed to reduce risk to acceptable levels.

Bladen et al's (2012) definitions serve as a good starting point to assist event managers in categorising the areas of their events where they need to undertake risk management. It also serves to help in analysing the risk elements that could cause harm to people. In other words, it is the identification of things that could go wrong (Tum et al, 2006) due to the events industry diversity and scope.

Due to the event industry being very diverse in its nature what it is clearly evident that risk management must have systematic health and safety frameworks and models in its pre-planning stage. This will also mean a coordinated approach with a number of key stakeholders as was discussed in Chapter 4. The risk management process are particularly susceptible to risks. As Bowdin et al (2011) points out this is due to unique venue, large crowds, new staff and volunteers, movement of equipment and general excitement are all a recipe for potential hazards that the event manager needs to consider in their planning.

What has been clearly established in these early stages that it is essential and integral part of the events management that event organisations formally need to plan for and develop strategies to deal with the possible consequences of unplanned events that may occur (Ferdinand and Kitchin, 2017). Also the event team must be able to show that effective risk management is being employed throughout the planning process of the event concept in its early stages, leading up to the event, during the event delivery and the post event debrief and evaluation. This further supported by Ferinand and Kitchin (2012) who put forward a similar view that a full risk assessment should be carried out for all events during their whole event life cycle and become an integral and strategic part of the organisational process and decision making (pg. 155).

Having established as part of Health and Safety the risk management element of a legal obligation is essential. With the wide a diverse scope of the industry how does this take place in ones such as localised events through to mega events? The health and safety has been described in a previous chapter as well as being defined within this. The application and understanding now serves as useful guidance in the steps that maybe entailed in carrying one out for an event at local level and then further with applied to bigger ones that may take place over a longer period of time.

Carrying out Risk Assessments for Local Events

Local events have been previously discussed in early chapters and therefore do not need defining for the understanding in carrying out a risk. What must be accepted though is that even if these events only take place over a short period of time such as few hours, half or a full day they need some sort of application of health, safety and risk management (HSRM) undertaken. Some of these areas have been previously discussed so a better understanding would best serve the event manager for the planning process would be the some of the steps that might be taken.

Bladen et al (2012) suggest a five step process (see figure 2) whereas the health and safety executive (2006) put forward a nine step process (see table 1). Each one has its own merits in its application, in particularly when it comes to events management. From an event managers perspective figure 2 (Bladen et al's, 2012) serves as a useful guidance. In localised event those involved in the development of the risk assessments will be a very small group of people and possibly one person tasked with the role. Using figure 2 this would enable an events practitioner to use the five step process in identifying basic issues surrounding their event, even the most minor of hazards and potentially how harmful they maybe to people attending

Figure 2. Five Steps to risk assessment (Adapted from Bladen et al, 2012)

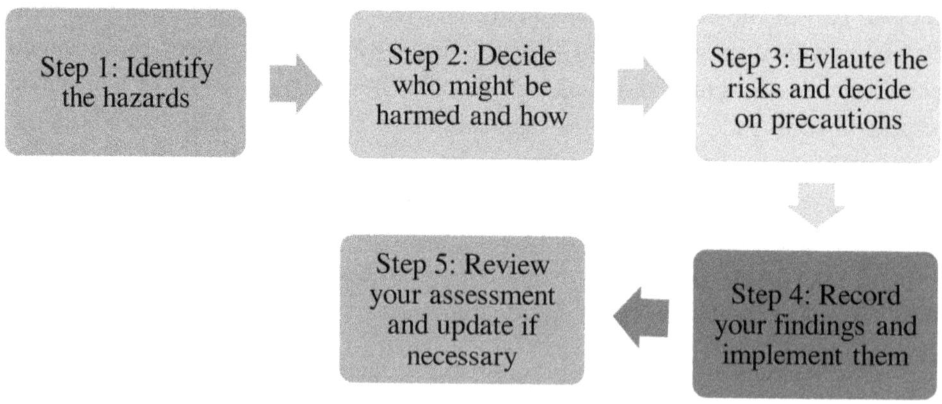

the event and also those who might be harmed in some way (Step 1 & 2). After undertaking the process they then would be able to decide what measures might need to be put in place for the risks/ hazards to avoided and also ensuring that they have been taken into consideration(Step 3). This could be in a localised event of someone managing people entering and exiting and summer fete in a village for example. After undertaking the initial risk assessment

Especially in such smaller events sometimes hazards can be overlooked due to the experience of the person undertaking the risk management process. What must be clearly understood within is that the hazard has the potential to cause harm and should be identified by understanding the environment or the context in which the event takes place (Beech, Kaiser and Kasper, 2014). Needless to say the identification of risk is necessary and the following guidance for smaller event organisers may wish to adopt the following suggested approach given by Beech et al (2014)

- Work breakdown structure (WBS, a decomposition of project into smaller components)
- Scenario development (what-if modelling)
- Brainstorming (Bruhwiler, 2011)
- Fault diagrams
- Statistical methods
- Testing a range of scenarios of potential risks and their effects
- Incident reports of similar events or different events at the same venue
- Also consultation (Bowdin et al, 2006)

Table 1. Nine Step Process in Risk Management (Adapted Health and Safety Executive, 2006)

Step 1	Understanding context: Consider event type, management, stakeholders and general environment
Step 2	Identifying risks: Look for hazards
Step 3	Decision: Decide who might be harmed and how
Step 4	Evaluating the risk: Evaluate the risks and decide whether the existing precautions are adequate or whether more should be done.
Step 5	Control: Control problems that may arise
Step 6	Mitigating actions: Consider mitigating actions
Step 7	Specific event risks: Consider specific event risks
Step 8	Recoding: Record your findings
Step 9	Review: Review your assessment and revise it if necessary

Even with the smallest events there needs to be a question raised "What is the likelihood?" The likelihood is the chance of 'it' happening and has to be estimated by the person undertaking it (Conway, 2009). The best guidance for small event organisers is to ensure that all health and safety management areas are covered and documented where it is possible. No matter what the scale of the event is the person responsible for providing a safe and healthy environment for those attending or involved no matter how long the duration is (Ritchie and Reid, 2017). In the case of smaller events as has already briefly been mentioned the health hazards should be the primary concern for the event organiser and the likelihood of it occurring should be considered. Allen, OToole, Harris and Mcdonnell (2007) recommend that a risk's likelihood of occurrence be rated on a five point scale from rare to almost certain. The consequence or severity of risks, on the other hand, will be given a rating of insignificant, minor, moderate, major or catastrophic. Table 2 gives some useful guidance towards how a risk assessment can be set out for an event. But what also must be noted that a risk is a subjective concept, and so rating scales are used by evet practitioners to try to create a more objective assessment of risk likelihood and consequence (Ritchie and Reid, 2017). Ritchie and Reid (2017) then offer some guidance on asking some questions to help determine the likelihood and consequence of something happening:

- What happens if the risk is not treated?
- Who will it affect?
- Whose responsibility is it to deal with the risk?
- What information do we need to treat it?
- What risks will important event stakeholders accept?

As Ritchie and Reid (2017) have already highlighted a risk is subjective and is open to the opinion of the person who is doing it in this case an individual for a small event however the most important thing is that there are a number of areas considered no matter how big the event is. Table 2 is almost a uniformed matric that is adopted by a number of organisations from local events through to mega event organisers.

Another reason for an event to take place is a charity or an organisation that might be about just putting on a social occasion for a gathering of people and therefore it is not profit driven and all about covering costs. This is also known as not for profit events.

Risk Management for Not for Profit Events

Other events have been previously been discussed in earlier chapters but not for those that are termed "not for profit?" These can be on the same scale as localised events to raise a village's profile, a school function, local fete or even a sporting event/ sports tournament. They can take the form of many different events with the sole purpose on being put on to potentially celebrate something and encouraging people to meet for a social occasion or even just meet up.

Whatever the purpose for this type the same consideration for risk assessment planning must take place as the scale of these events can vary in size, scope and also the number of attendees. The prevention and mitigation are the first line of defence for event organisers (Ferdinand and Kitchin, 2017) in these type of events. Even at the initial planning phase where the specifications for the not for profit event are determined, specifying the activities that will occur and how the resources will be organised (Silver, 2008). If the event is of a larger scale to improve event operations, the event practitioner for these types of events should try and assemble a group of people with varying experiences that can be drawn upon that can assist in identifying the risks and develop the risk management and evacuation plans (Glodblatt, 1997). By having a group of people in this instance will enable a mixture of views, experiences and knowledge to be drawn upon and it will potentially see something that may appear safe to some event staff but may contain possibly hidden dangers (Bowdin et al, 2011). Therefore the process is must be of sequential nature, yet must be iterative in practice (Rutherford-Silvers, 2008). The process, no matter what size of the event is, must be proactive and cyclical, facilitating communication, forecasting and forward planning by the person in charge, or the collective group with the responsibility.

Berlonghi (1009) offers some guidance on several generic strategies that can be employed for events to follow:

- Avoidance; the hazard, such a programme of activity or venue, should be eliminated.
- Reduction; some hazards can be minimised or kept to an acceptable level through better management, training or operations, or actions focused on reducing potential severity of damage or losses.
- Diffusion; spreading risks among stakeholders or over time and space.
- Reallocation; risks can be reallocated completely, as where a parent body or municipality absorbs risks for specific events; user have to sign waivers.

The guidance for some of the strategies that Berlonghi (1990) serve as a useful guidance to event practitioners to consider some of the ways to look at how to best approach their risk assessments and eliminate issues. Once controls have been proposed event managers can revisit the documents and make adjustments and changes to each risk based on the significance of the controls proposed, their reduction of likelihood and/ or reduction in consequence (Van der Wagen and White, 2010). As we have looked at there are a number of steps that can be taken by those who have suggested them (Bladen et al, 2012; HSE, 2006).

The most important thing from these steps being identified, for example the five step process and that the event manager uses these to consider and potentially control some of those risks/ hazards using a methodical and an easy to use process. Furthermore it must be acknowledged that the event manager must allocate the correct resources to each of the steps. What must be acknowledged many of the risk associated with events can vary in scale and specific to the type of event? The risks associated with these vary according to the nature of the event (HSE,1999). Whichever the case that might be what is generally agreed that sometimes at an event may be a result of ignoring the risks before the event. For this reason, the risk management must be tracked across all areas of event management (Bowdin et al, 2008).

What can be seen, even with not for profit events, that all areas of event need to be considered no matter what the size and magnitude they are. In much bigger events such as major events with mass numbers and potential issues and also security this adds another dimension to these to consider in an event managers planning. Therefore working closely with a number of key stakeholders in the event management process will have to take place for all the stakeholders involved.

Risk Management for Major Events

Considerations for risk management could even be more important than planning and designing events (Boo and Gu, 2010). Philip and Kiren (1990) studied this process as a result because of a notable major event. They suggested that the event was profitable because of the risk management program that was undertake. Chang and Singh (1990) suggested a two-step risk management which could be applied to the event. However with greater analysis this has become outdated as the events industry has moved on. This is clearly evident from the five step process presented by Bladen et al (2012) and also the HSE (1999) nearly one and two decades on from Chang and Singhs (1990) application to the industry. Leopkey and Parent (2009a) believe that the use of proper strategies for risk reduction can directly influence the organisations overall performance and the success of the event. Strategies used for controlling risks may require additional documents, such as an emergency evacuation plan, crowd management plan or crisis communication plan (Ritchie and Reid, 2017).

Risk communication involves both information and consultation, requiring two-way capability for giving and getting messages about the entire scope of the event and its risk management activities, actions and outcomes Rutherford Silvers, 2008). Effective risk communication should facilitate this collaboration and the acquisition of proactive data that helps predict and prepare for risks and getting risk messages before, not after, something has happened (Smith and Merritt, 2002). When dealing with large crowds, in particular at major events effective communication is essential to keep people informed of risk messages and the potential of issues arising and also the management of them. The most important of aspect of crowd management involves making accurate estimate of the number of attendees (Bowdin et al, 2010; Silvers, 2004).

A good communication process is critical to the effectiveness of risk monitoring and control strategies, and must facilitate the proper flow and Kendrick (2003) suggests one as is demonstrated in Figure 3. He further highlights it must be timely, accurate, and to the point, and once corrective action has been taken, this must be communicated to internal and external staff, suppliers, and stakeholders (Kendrick, 2003). Regularly scheduled meetings will support these objectives as progress, changes, and emerging risks can be reviewed and addressed.

Figure 3. Communication Process (Adapted from Kendrick, 2003)

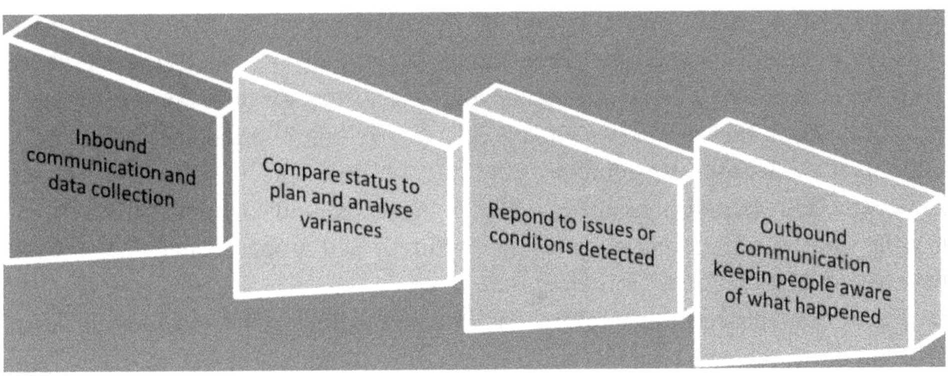

When crowds/ are large numbers of people attend a major event it is essential, as it has already been mentioned, that you must to try and pre-empt any potential problems before the event takes place? Many crowd control issues arise from the inadequate risk management by the event company (Bowdin et al, 2010). Abbott and Geddie (2001) suggest that there three stages in a crowd control plan pre-crisis and post-crisis. During the pre-crisis stage the event manager will consider certain preventative tactics to avoid crowd control problems (such as staff training, facilities management and the use of a control centre to aid communication. A crowd-related risk assessment will be produced at this stage (Bladen et al, 2012). The second stage -the crisis stage – begins when the preventative measures fail. During this stage, practical crowd control measures, such as clear evacuation procedures and clam personnel are essential- as is a proactive response before the situation escalates. The final stage- the post crisis stage-involves the review and evaluation of the strategy after the event. A full review should be completed by the organiser to ascertain whether security and personnel responded effectively and efficiently, and to identify key issues or problems that may arise again in the future (Bladen et al, 2012). There have been many incidents, in particular in the United Kingdom (UK), where poor communication has resulted in crowd management problems. The "Fish Quay Festival" that was formerly sponsored by the telecommunications company 'Orange' which resulted in mass surges nearly crushing people where the event managers didn't build into their risk management detail this happening. The impact of poor communications about the flow of people in the area had a major impact on the number people moving through a Quayside area that was too narrow to cope with the volume of people. There have been further incidents, not only in the UK. The Haj Festival that is held annually in Saudi Arabia has a long history of poor crowd management since 1987 through to when the latest data was published in 2006 where there have a total of 4,835 deaths or injuries from varying degrees (Cabinet Office, 2009) over a period 19 years. What can be seen that effective planning in crowd management is essential in particular for major events where there are going to be a large number of attendees. Most event organisers create a production book that includes contracts, plans, meeting minutes, correspondence, and copies of licenses, or approvals that may be necessary to confirm authority and instructions (Rutherford-Silvers, 2008). What also must be noted from this is that the success of an event depends on the timely and proper management of the volumes of information surrounding the event.

The formal process and volume of communicating risks includes also the distribution of the risk plan (Bowdin et al, 2011). What also must be noted from this that in a fluid event management environment, a fixed plan may be quickly out of date? Therefore event organisers need to ensure that all elements of event communications in crowd management are fairly robust in the planning stage and that they consider as many probable issues that can arise during an event. And has been highlighted that all risks are reported in a timely fashion as and when they occur. This should be coupled with standard, yet customised, reporting procedure an also reduce the risk of an ineffective communication, what also must be remembered that communication in large scaled events are not about those delivering the events but also about those who are attending as well. Needless this type of communication can also be how the people attending the event are informed through things such as signage and keeping them also informed whey they are at events venue.

There are numerous other threats or hazards that can the event manager or company, all of which can potentially be harmful and a risk and some of these are listed:

- Protests
- Traffic
- Unruly fans
- Alcohol
- Terrorism

However some of these will be discussed with regards to Mega Events which can be, like major events, very complex in their risk management due to the size, scale and duration.

Risk Management in Mega Events

With risk management in mega events many studies have focused on hosting the Olympic Games (Neirotti & Hilliard, 2006; Taylor & Toohey, 2007; Toohey & Taylor, 2008). However, most of their focus on the main judgements of respondents regarding the riskiness of events. For example Taylor and Tooheys (2006) focus explored whether terrorism-related safety concerns influence attendee's decision-making; the impact of tightened security measures and their satisfaction. They showed that, if friends and family showed concern about their loved ones attendance at the event, this was important for planning future sports events (Taylor & Toohey,2006a).

This example presented about Toohey and Taylor (2006a) highlights that terrorism has now become a highly important area in the consideration for event managers when it comes to risk management for attendees. In particular sporting events primarily is the risk of terrorism and tightened security measures, and even more so the focuses since post 9/11 of attendees attitudes and behaviours. Clearly today security is an essential and a big part of risk of planning and key part of event operations and logistics (Getz, 2012). Understanding crowd emotions and behaviour is essential for most events, with the threat of terrorism as has been previously highlighted (Toohey & Taylor 2006a) at major events being an added worry. Tarlow (2002) in Getz (2012) highlights in his book Event Risk Management and Safety, drew attention to the links between terrorism, specifically why they make inviting targets:

- Proximity of events and event venues to major transportation routes and centres
- Potentially large-scale business and tourism disruption from cancellation or postponement
- Media attention is immediate, on-site;
- Customers at many events are unknown in crowds.

Also because of the heightened increase threat of terrorism risk management in this area is now at the forefront in mega-event planning and has resulted in range of new security measures for spectators and tougher safety standards for the event organiser (Toohey & Taylor, 2008). To support his further terrorist- based risk associated attack with spectating in the 21st century is not without substance, because there have been 168 terrorist attacks related to sport between 1974 and 2004 (Clark, 2004; Kennelly, 2005; Toohey & Taylor, 2008) . The figures demonstrate that there is a clear link between terrorism and events as was further highlighted in Manchester O2 Arena where 23 people were killed during a pop concert in 2017 (The Sun, 2019). Since such incidents careful and well thought out planning has to now take place to ensure that there are sufficiently trained staff to deal with such areas. There has been a security standard industry association license so that such staffs are trained to undertake roles at events. This area will always remain a contentious area of discussion and continuous analysis in the way of how it will be risk managed. Lessons will always be learned from areas that have gone before. The most important issue for the event manager is to consider and write into their risk management the probability of areas that potentially have to be taken into thought out in the area.

What clearly becomes apparent that this now has to be built into major and mega event risk assessments that such probable causes are written into their documents due to the size and scope of each event, but also some of the key stakeholders such as the emergency services and the military are particularly involved in the planning due to the threat of terror.

Mega events to this day, due the terrorist threat, have an extensive police and military presence which eliminates these probabilities from happening. These are now seen as essential part of planning, security and the delivery of events of such a magnitude. It is also important to understand the chain of command when emergency's services are involved in the event delivery. This can be outside the control of the event management staff, who would be purely be in an advisory capacity (Bowdin et al, 2012). This what is put forward with so many stakeholders involved as a multi-agency approach and without a doubt will be required for this type of event, also in such areas where crowds may influenced with alcohol or drugs which also result unruly behaviour by attendees.

The management Alcohol and drugs makes up an important aspect of control systems that need to be implemented in order to maintain a safe and comfortable atmosphere at an event (Bladen et al, 2012). Events featuring alcohol consumption, dependent on the type of event their audience may face problems as unruly crowd behaviour which have also been shown in events (Carlson et al, 2010; Harris et al, 2014). Getz (2005) lists the following risks associated with alcohol sales at events:

- Personal injuries and criminal acts owing to drunkenness
- Additional insurance costs against possibility of lawsuits
- Additional security and clean-up costs
- Major financial losses from lawsuits
- Vandalism
- Image problems and resultant lost patronage
- Attracting the wrong target segments.

With these types of risks it has to be acknowledged that the actions of attendees can be somewhat unpredictable and therefore where there is an opportunity for these to be consumed or not prevented that the event manager ensures that these are included in their risk management document. If they can, event organisers carefully consider the distribution, sales and consumption of alcohol for instance (Abbot and Geddie, 2001) and put security measures in place for drug consumption. Getz (2005) puts forward a view that if event wishes to sell alcohol for example the event organiser should also have am alcohol risk management system in place, including practising responsible service of alcohol (Harris et al, 2014) and this can be potentially monitored from a central point such as a central control or command centre. This is would be common in mega events due to the duration of these.

Central control or command centres enable event organisers to maintain control and coordination throughout the duration of an event (Ritchie and Reid, 2017). Berlonghi (195) states that the centre has the responsibility to coordinate security efforts a, as well as making evacuation announcements when an event upstaged by an emergency. Also the centre, when there is temporary CCTV can have an overview of what is going on dealing with the potential unruly behaviour of attendees. This very similar to the Notting Hill carnival in London whom also use a control centre to monitor activities via CCTV as well as deal as at the carnival site to deal with potential unruly behaviour.

One more areas to consider with such event as the Notting hill carnival as Ritchie and Reid (2017) point out is where noise levels are high as these can also be associated with criminal activities in the past, including stabbings, shootings, drug distribution and drug taking. Therefore as well as having these written into the risk assessment as Abbott and Geddie (2001) share that event organisers may want to have policies concerning drug and alcohol consumption and sales should be created to avoid having the events image tarnished by alcohol-related problems.

To manage potential drug and alcohol related problems and minimise the impact on an event or to cover this element in risk management Harris et al (2014) provides event organisers with some guidance:

- Entry controls: to the event venues or parts of the venue where alcohol is served. These can include point monitoring, bag searches, ID scanning and capping entry.
- Alcohol service controls: such as restrictions on alcohol strength, glass serving containers and limits on the number of drinks bought at any one time.
- Attendee/ patron management: including provision of free food and water, CCTV, educational campaigns and progressive shutdown of venues in order to reduce anti-social behaviour.
- Site/ venue layout and design: including adequate number of facilities, chill-out or alcohol-free areas, sufficient space, lighting and heating which can prevent anti-social behaviour.
- Regulatory and enforcement practices: including defined trading hours, compliance checks by police or licensing authorities, targeted enforcement or venue practices.

The careful management of these potential risks and well thought out preventative measures will enable an event organiser. Accepting and understanding this type of risk is another way of dealing with risks-called risk retention-but risks should be evaluated before they are accepted (Beech, Kaiser and Kasper, 2014). They further go onto highlight reduce the impact of potential damage by selecting the least damaging option and documenting the steps in the risk assessment then the event organiser has recognised and taken whereby the risk is diminished (Beech, Kaiser and Kasper, 2014). To avoid incidents as a result of risks. If incidents do occur, prevent them from becoming crises. If a crisis occurs, minimise the impact on the event, the event organisation and the stakeholders and, especially in major and mega events, form a crisis management team (Bruhwiler, 2011).

Forming a crisis management team is a useful option when it comes to risk management. Also in doing so it will also enable the option for risk transference, in particularly for events of this size. By reallocating of risks to another contracted company to perform certain tasks and responsibilities means it is covered under their insurance. This may involve external security companies, equipment suppliers in such areas as concerts. In Australia for examples most performance groups are required to have public liability insurance before they can take part in an event (Allen et al, 2008). Insurances an essential part of event management therefore by sharing this cost or a liability at an event elevates pressures on evet organisations where this maybe potentially specified when using external contractors. This will also form a part of the event evaluation on the effectiveness and impact of the provider/ contractor or more importantly were they needed?

The overall success of an event and its risk management process is the continuous monitoring and evaluation of every aspect of what is happening and taking place.

By undertaking such areas can be seen as control strategies on ensuring a successful event is delivered now and for the future. Therefore this is an essential part of planning and for future events being delivered.

CONCLUSION

What is clearly evident that risk management forms as an essential part in event delivery no matter what size the event is? With meticulous though and planning throughout the initial ideas of the event concept (type of event) then all the factors leading up to the event, the event being delivered and post the event this area needs effective planning and consideration of every element. These areas have been highlighted in particular for the attendees and also those who are delivering the actual event itself. The most important element of risk management is the event organisation has a duty of care to ensure that they have considered as many possibilities or the probable cause of risks and hazards for the type of event that is being delivered. As well as this they have will helped to reduce or minimise any potential liability whilst the event is being delivered and also post the event as well.

Practical Events Management

North Shields Fish Quay Festival began in 1987 as a community event with a blessing of the fleet while local talent was called on to entertain the crowds.Then

Figure 4. Case Study: The Fish Quay Festival

the festival began to grow and by 2001 it had become the Window on the WHuge stages were erected and the large crowds brought big name acts like Jools Holland, Take That, The Levellers, The Wailers, Bob Geldof and Hear' Say. At its height more than 200 workers were needed to organise and staff it and national and multinational companies stumped up sponsorship. In just three days in 2001 the event brought around £11m into the local economy.But the WOW festival was scrapped by former Conservative mayor Chris Morgan in August 2002 when he realised costs were spiraling out of control. Around £350,000 dedicated to the event was taken away and it was re-launched as the Fish Quay Family Festival with a budget of just £70,000.

Figure 5. Fish Quay Festival in 1987

The downsized festival also brought in tens of thousands of pounds to the local economy. There was a mix of street theatre, market stalls, fairground rides and live music on the quay.A thanksgiving service for the fishing fleet began proceedings, followed by a parade of boats, a pageant and a parade featuring youngsters from 20 schools.However, in 2006 North Tyneside Council decided not to hold the Fish Quay Festival. The reason given was health and safety concerns about visitors coming to the town when long-term redevelopment work was taking place.A council report recommended that the future of the festival should be heritage based.

The Mouth of The Tyne festival currently continues the local festival tradition, held jointly between Tynemouth and South Shields. This summer there will be three concerts, all in the spectacular setting of Tynemouth Priory and Castle from Friday July 12 to Sunday July 14.The Friday evening concert will be headlined by 1980s group The Human League. On Saturday evening James Morrison returns

Figure 6. Steve Harley at the Festival in 1992

following his sell out show three years ago and The Wonder Stuff will headline the Sunday afternoon show.

REFERENCES

Abbot, J. L. (2001). Event and venue management: Minimising liability through crowd management techniques. *Event Management*, *6*(4), 259–270. doi:10.3727/152599500108751417

Allen, I., O'Toole, W., Harris, R., & McDonnell, I. (2008). Festival and Event management (4th ed.). Brisbane: John Wiley & Sons Australia.

Beech, J., Kaiser, S., & Kaspar, R. (2014). *Event Risk Management. In The Business of Event Management* (pp. 181–198). Person.

Berlonghi, A. (1990). *Special Event Risk Management Manual.* Mansfield, OH: Bookmasters.

Berlonghi, A. (1994). *The Special Event Risk Management Manual.* Academic Press.

Bladen, C., Kennel, J., Abson, E., & Wilder, N. (2012). Event Health, safety and risk Management. In *Events Management: Introduction*. Routledge.

Boo, S., & Gu, H. (2010). Risk Perception of Mega-events. *Journal of Sport & Tourism, 15*(2), 131–161. doi:10.1080/14775085.2010.498257

Bowdin, G., Allen, J., O'Toole, W., Harris, R., & McDonnell, I. (2006). Events Management (2nd ed.). Amsterdam: Elsevier.

Bowdin, G., Allen, J., O'Toole, W., Harris, R., & McDonnell, I. (2008). Risk Management and Legal Issues. In Events Management (2nd ed.). Elsevier.

Bowdin, G., Allen, J., O'Toole, W., Harris, R., & McDonnell, I. (2011). Risk Management Process. In Events Management (3rd ed.). Elsevier.

British Standards Institution (BSI). (2002). *Project Risk Management- Application Guidelines*. London: BSI.

Bruhwhiler, B. (2011). *Risikomanagement als Fuhrungsaqufgabe* (3rd ed.). Bern: Haupt-Verlag.

Cabinet Office. (2009). *Understanding crowd behaviours; support evidence*. The Cabinet Office London. www.assets.publishing.service.gov.uk

Chang, P. C., & Singh, K. K. (1990). Risk Management for mega-events. *Tourism Management, 11*(2), 45–52. doi:10.1016/0261-5177(90)90007-V

Conway, D. (2009). Health and Safety. In *The Event Managers Bible: The complete guide to planning and organising a voluntary or public event*. How to Books.

Ferdinand, N., & Kitchin, P. J. (2012). *Events Management; An international approach*. London: Sage.

Ferdinand, N., & Kitchin, P. J. (2017). *Risk Management*. Events Management; An international approach. London. *Sage,* 221–240.

Getz, D. (2002). Why *Festivals Fail. Event Management*, *7*(4), 209–219. doi:10.3727/152599502108751604

Getz, D. (2005). *Event Management and Event Tourism* (2nd ed.). New York: Cognizant Group.

Getz, D. (2012). *Planning and management of events* (2nd ed.). Event Studies, Theory, Policy for Planned Events.

Getz, D., & Page, S. J. (2016). *Planning and Management of events. In Event Studies* (pp. 348–349). Theory, Research and Policy for Planned Events.

Glodblatt, J. J. (1997). *Special events: Best practices in Modern Event Management* (2nd ed.). Wiley & Sons.

Harris, R., Edwards, D., & Homel, P. (2014). *Managing alcohol and drugs in event and venue settings:* The Australisn case. *Event Management, 18*(4), 457–470. doi: 10.3727/152599514X14143427352238

Health and Safety Executive. (1999). *The event safety guide*. Norwich HSE Books.

Health and Safety Executive. (2006). *Five steps to Risk Management*. London: HSE.

Kendrick, T. (2003). *Identifying and Managing Project Risk*. AMACOM.

Neirotti, L. D., & Hilliard, T. (2006). Impact of Olympic spectator safety perception and security concerns on travel decisions. *Tourism Review International, 10*(4), 269–284. doi:10.3727/154427206779367109

O'Toole, W., & Mikolatis, P. (2002). *Corporate Event project Management*. New York: Wiley.

Philip & Kiren, C. K. (1990). Risk management for mega-events: The 1988 Olympic Winter Games. *Tourism Management, 3*, 45.

Ritchie, B. W., & Reid, S. (2017). Risk Management. Events Management: An International Approach, 211-240.

Rutherford-Silvers, J. (2008). The role of risk management of meeting and events. In Risk Management for Meeting and Events. Routledge.

Rutherford-Silvers, J. (2008). The role of risk management of meeting and events. In *Risk Management for Meeting and Events*. Routledge.

Silver, J. R. (2008). *Risk Management for Meetings and Events*. Oxford, UK: Butterworth-Heinemann. doi:10.1016/B978-0-7506-8057-8.50009-2

Smith, P. G., & Merritt, G. M. (2002). *Proactive Risk Management: Controlling Uncertainty in Product Development*. Productivity Press.

Taylor, T., & Toohey, K. (2006a). Security, perceived safety, and event event attendee enjoyment at the 2003 Rugy World Cup. *Tourism Review International, 10*(4), 100–209. doi:10.3727/154427206779367127

Taylor, T., & Toohey, K. (2007). Perceptions of terrorism threats at the 2004 Olympic Games: Implications for sports event. *Journal of Sport & Tourism, 12*(2), 99–114. doi:10.1080/14775080701654754

Toohey, K., & Taylor, T. (2008). Meg events, fear and risk: Terrorism at the Olympic Games. *Journal of Sport Management*, *22*(4), 100–209. doi:10.1123/jsm.22.4.451

Van Der Wagen, L., & White, L. (2010). *Safety and Security Risks. In Events Management; for tourism, cultural, business and sporting events* (4th ed.). Pearson.

Chapter 2
Management of Health and Safety Risks at Large Events:
Process, Procedures, and Factors

Sumesh Singh Dadwal
Northumbria University, London, UK

Dhanwant Dadwal
Dadwal Consultants London Ltd., UK

ABSTRACT

This chapter details and guides managers and researchers to consider organisational culture, risk management systems, procedures, principles, and processes to manage larger events successively and effectively without any potential tragedies, harms, and risks. It begins with the conceptual understanding of events and how the event organising involves managing health and safety risks. Health and safety management in such situations consists of organised efforts and procedures for identifying workplace hazards and reducing accidents and exposure to harmful situations and substances. The events are organised with different purposesm and each event has a unique blending of durations, seating, management, and people. This is further followed by risk management planning, which assists event organisers in devising and conducting events in the safest possible manner while mitigating losses. HSE England commissioned a study in 2012 and found a range of potential risks and remedies at major events. The main risk identified were design and construction, public health and safety risks, airborne and communicable diseases, non-infectious risk, respiratory diseases, road traffic accident, crowd control, strain on healthcare, workplace violence, fires, etc. Managing a safe event involves planning, assessing risks, precautions measure and corrective and perverting actions, contingency,

DOI: 10.4018/978-1-7998-3230-0.ch002

emergency planning and procedures, effective communications, managing crowd and resources, review, and reflection. The primary legislation covering occupational health and safety in Britain is the Health and Safety at Work Act 1974, which makes employers responsible for the management of health and safety. It sets out the general duties which employers have towards employees and members of the public, and employees have to themselves and to each other. The last section discusses main principles of a H&S risk management policy followed by some case studies.

INTRODUCTION

Health and safety are defined as 'the laws, rules, and principles that are intended to keep people safe from injury or disease at work and in public places (Cambridge dictionary, 2019). Health and safety management is ' Organized efforts and procedures for identifying workplace hazards and reducing accidents and exposure to harmful situations and substances. It also includes training of personnel in accident prevention, accident response, emergency preparedness, and use of protective clothing and equipment (Business dictionary, 2019). A risk at an event is ' effects of uncertainty on objectives (financial, social, environmental, health, and safety), to varying levels (strategic, organization, or project) and likelihoods' (Reid & Ritchie, 2011)

As an event organiser, you have a duty of care – to both your attendees and your staff. The larger your event, the more important health and safety, but even for small events it should still be a consideration.

Event as a Concept

An event is composed of set of activities with specific purpose goals and needs of the attendees Thus an event is an 'organized occasion such as meeting, music testable, product/brand promotion, convention, conference, exhibition, special event, wedding, social gathering or gala dinner, and so on; and it is made up of several related activities and functions with the purpose of attending the specific needs of the attendees' (Bikash, 2013, Julian & Dadwal et al 2019). An event is a process with 'a beginning and an end that happens at a given place, time and circumstances'(Levy, Bogin, Gretz, Aharonov, & Slonim, 2018) and (Julian & Dadwal et l 2019). Each event has a unique blending of durations, seating, management and people (Vassilopoulos 2005, cited in (Bikash, 2013)). The events are organised with different purposes such as' touristic or other purposes such as entertainment, relaxations, competitions, customs & cultural celebration or brand building or the need to raise funds for charity, public/government purpose and so on (Julian & Dadwal et al 2019). The events can be planned or unplanned events.

The planned events are 'created with a pre-planned social, cultural, economic, or environmental purpose. Such events involve the design and implementation of themes, settings, consumables, services, and programs that suggest, facilitate or constrain experiences for participants, guests, spectators, and other stakeholders. Every event experience is personal and unique, arising from the interactions of setting, program, and people' (Getz, 2018, Julian & Dadwal et al 2019).On the other hand, the unplanned events are 'random, spontaneous and unpredictable activities probably set in motion by people (Agitators, publicity agents or social activists). Once it starts, the actions that follow are uncertain (Getz, 2018, Julian & Dadwal et l 2019).

Each type of event involves a range of risks including health and safety risks.

The larger events have more risks; however, the small events may also involve many risks. Also by size, contents and forms etc the events can have various risks. Depending upon the types of risks the event planners have to manage risks at the events. So various risk factors also depends upon the type of events, such as 'Local or community events (music programs, community meeting, fundraising program, BBQ parties), Major events, Hallmark events (Kumbh Mela in India, Haj Visits, Carnival in Rio or London), Mega-events (2012 London Olympics and Queen's Diamond Jubilee celebrations), Cultural events (wedding events, commercial music festivals, Art festivals Chinese New Year, Holi Festival, Kumbh Mela, Carnival of Rio de Janeiro, St. Patrick's Day Festival,) Sports events (Football World cup, Olympics, The Ashes), Business events (product launches, making publicity stunts,) (Bikash, 2013, Julian & Dadwal et l 2019).

Event Management as a Process

Event Management is 'a process of planning, organising, coordinating, executing various activities at an event with effective use of all the event resources to meet the specific goals and objective of the event' (Bikash, 2013, Julian & Dadwal et l 2019). The health and safety risk planning involves a pre-event process of identifying the target audiences and risks, planning, and scheduling for activities and budgets and other resources. The risk management involves coordination and linking different actors, agents and supplier organisations who come together to successfully complete an event. The evaluation is the post-event process and reflecting on the risks forecasted with an actually achieved goal is an important part of risk management. An event is a 'project' or a temporary cluster of industries (Benedicta, Rani, & Longhi, 2011, Julian & Dadwal et l 2019). Thus, models and theories of project risk management can be used as a basis for effective event management. 'Both projects and events have temporary in nature & life i.e. Both have short life from start to finish, and most people employed at events or projects are of temporary nature for a limited or Adhoc time. This adhocracy brings issues of managing uniform standards of quality, quantity, and costs, etc (Julian & Dadwal et l 2019). Thus risk and 'issues of events and tourism management can be agreed by taking a combination project management, clustered development and system approaches to the management' (Julian & Dadwal. 2019).

Tourism and events production 'process include a range of activities, products, and services offered by coordinated suppliers and agents' (Bénédicte, Rani, & Longhi, 2011, Julian & Dadwal, 2019). Thus proper 'coordination of such a diverse set of suppliers, operations, processes, activities, and products' (Julian & Dadwal et l 2019) can mitigate a number of risks. The 'use of technology is a viable option and strategy for tourism and event planners. The emerging technologies like Cloud technology, Cognatic & Artificial intelligence, Blockchain, artificial & Virtual reality, Live apps, etc. has huge potential to change the events and tourism industry'(Julian & Dadwal et l 2019. The use of technology and ICT can be very useful to integrate different components of a project sniff then link those components with stakeholders' expectations (Bénédicte, Rani, & Longhi, 2011, Julian & Dadwal et l 2019).

Risk Conceptualisation

A Risk is related to future activity related to a process that has consequences with respect to something that humans value (planned values, objectives, negative consequences, etc) (Aven, 2016). The risk can be in all fields, whether finance, safety engineering, health, transportation, security or supply chain management and it results in negative consequences. Thus risk is consequences of the activity and associated uncertainties, the possibility of an unfortunate occurrence, potential for realisation of unwanted negative consequences of an event, exposure to a loss which is uncertain, the deviation from a reference value, the effect of uncertainty on objectives, etc (Aven, 2016). A risk could be measured as triplet made up of *C*, *P*, *K*; where *C* is consequences (damage, loss, etc), *P is* a measure of uncertainty or probability and *K* the background knowledge that supports *C* and *P* (Aven, 2016).

Health and Safety Risk at Events

Events attract a huge crowd within a limited defined space and time so have high potential health and safety risks. For successful, safe and suitable risk organisations the organisations have to consider a range of occupational health and safety requirements, the legal duty of care, and the capacity of organizations to deal with risks(Reid & Ritchie, 2011). Risk management planning assists event organisers in devising and conducting events in the safest possible manner, while mitigating losses (Reid & Ritchie, 2011). The events involves engagement and coordination of a number of stakeholders and host organizations (including accommodation providers, government agencies, entrepreneurs, non-profit organizations such as sporting and cultural groups, etc.), as well as industry sectors (including venues, construction, staging, accommodation, entertainment, transport, tours, retail, and food/beverages)(Reid & Ritchie, 2011). All the stakeholders should jointly develop and interactively implement a risk management strategy . as per therapies of reasoned actions and theories of planned behaviour, the individual's attitude, behaviours, norms and a range of phycological factors can influence the adoption of risk planning activities. The other factors include lack of money, lack of knowledge/expertise, and lack of responsibility for dealing with natural hazard risk, organizational systems, organisational size, type, culture, structure, resources, leadership, and communication (Reid & Ritchie, 2011).

A risk as is ' effects of uncertainty on objectives (financial, social, environmental, health, and safety), to varying levels (strategic, organization, or project) and likelihoods' (Reid & Ritchie, 2011). Risk, in A Risk at events, is defined as "any condition or occurrence that might affect the outcome of an event or event activities and might expose an event organization to loss measured in terms of probability and consequences" (Silvers, 2008, p. 4, cited by Reid & Ritchie, 2011). The risk can be security and safety, health risks, life risks, stakeholders' relationship risks, climate change risks, insurance crisis, and so on.

The risk management is 'a process that involves assessing all possible risks to the event and its stakeholders and then strategically avoiding, preventing, reducing, diffusing, reallocating, legalizing, or using relationship management to mitigate the identified risks' (Leopkey and Parent 2009, cited in Reid & Ritchie, 2011).

Citing the Australian and New Zealand International Standards (2009) (AS/NZS ISO 31000:2009), Reid & Ritchie, (2011) argued that an effective risk management should be a comprehensive, logical, integrative and 'systematic method of establishing the context, identifying, analysing, evaluating, treating, monitoring, and communicating risks associated with any activity or function'. Thus in line of this definition, the Event organisers should need an understanding of the context & type of event, management structure and resources, organizational culture, and stakeholder involvement, to provide insight into event risk exposure and their consequences (Allen, O'Toole, Harris, & McDonnell, 2008 cited in Reid & Ritchie,2011).

A hazard is something that can cause harm, e.g. electricity, chemicals, working up a ladder, noise, a keyboard, a bully at work, stress, etc. A risk is a chance, high or low, that any hazard will actually cause somebody harm. For example, working alone away from your office can be a hazard. Health and well-being in the workplace have become common topics in the mainstream media (Coleman, 1997), in practitioner-oriented magazines and journals King, 1995; Neville, 1998) and, increasingly, in scholarly research journals (Smith, Kaminstein, & Makadok,1995).

Major Health and Safety Risk at Events

Big events, like sports games, exhibitions, entertaining shows, recruitments, garden parties, temple fairs and parades which involve public participants are events has often very high density of people in a small area at a particular time. 'Basing on the uncertainties from its publicity, mass participation, long time span, high input cost and other properties, it is necessary to run risk control for big event' (Shangjun & Xinjian, 2012). Due to the diversity of visitors by age, occupation, personal behaviour, lifestyle and other socio-cultural and psychological differences of the participants, the management becomes complicated. As conflicts would easily be turned into fights and brawling, stampedes etc. Many factors like diverse Mass of participants, The temporary building of sites, Suddenness and Uncertainty of accidents, Terrorist attacks etc some subsystems of overall events that need to be managed for the risks. Some major tragedies at events include: stampede (such had happened in the annual Muslim Pilgrimage of Mecca), terrorist attacks (such had happened in the 1972 Munich Olympics), Fire (such had happened in the 2005 Aichi Expo), natural disasters (such had happened in 2003 as the spread of virus SARS brought a huge negative impact to the Chinese MICE industry). The causes of all those tragedies could be aligned to the incomplete management of forecasting, the lack of emergency equipment and facilities, and the breakdown of venue facilities, man-made damages, and natural disasters and so on(Shangjun & Xinjian, 2012).

HSE England commissioned a study in 2012 and found a range of potential risks and remedies at major events (HSE, 2012). The main risk identified were design & Construction, Public health and safety risks, Airborne and communicable diseases, Non-Infectious Risk, Respiratory Diseases, Road Traffic accident, Crowd control, Strain on health care,, Workplace violence, Fires: etc, There are often concerns regarding competent persons required for risk assent and management at major events. The competence train for employees and volunteers is one of the important strategies to manage and mitigate H&S risks at the events.

The following section discusses the risks in more detail.

Design and Construction

The define of the event site and construction has been noted as a major potential risk of health and safety at the events. The literature shows that lack of robust design of construction sites, temporary stadia, structural faults, personal protective equipment (PPE), poor signage and walkways etc. for example, a tower at the Atlanta Olympic Stadium caused a cantilevered canopy to collapse, killing a construction worker, similar issues were identified at the Sydney Olympic Games and commonwealth games in India. mitigate such risks, includes following codes of striatal deign, providing health and safety awareness sessions/training of workers, H&S monitoring and reporting procedures, health surveillance, ensuring availability of PPE, effective leadership, worker engagement, control of contractors, and encouraging a positive safety culture, etc (HSE, 2012).

Public Health and Safety Risks

A range of waterborne and airborne communicable disease is another risk at a major event. The intervention could include, maintenance of cooling towers, use of technology such as geographical information systems by local councils to gather intelligence, education of facility owners, and surveillance programs with a particular emphasis on inspections and microbiological testing (prior and during the event, and also of decorative fountains & swimming pools)and antimalaria campaigns etc.

Airborne and Communicable Diseases

Due to the volume and movement of the people, There will be a high level of risk of airborne disease at mass gatherings. For instance, an early review of communicable diseases in competitive sports carried out between 1966 and 1993 identified only 38 reports of a disease outbreak(HSE, 2012). an outbreak of measles during the International Special Olympics in the US in 1991 and the 2006 football World Cup in Germany. Other examples of infectious diseases identified included a case of meningitis outbreak during a European Youth Olympic Sports festival, meningococcal meningitis at a UK rugby match etc (HSE, 2012). An Epidemic intelligence programme that could identify, assess, verify and investigate potential health risks could be an important solution. Further, establishing appropriate mechanisms to allow surveillance & immediate reporting of communicable diseases; staff training in collecting and analysing surveillance data; public awareness and immunized against vaccine-preventable diseases could be effective measures for controlling airborne and communicable diseases(HSE, 2012).

Non-Infectious Risk

Exposure to extreme weather conditions such as heat, exhaustion/stroke, sunburns and dehydration, cold, water /humidity, etc has also negative effects on attendees and employees. A number of incidents such as the volleyball venue during the Atlanta Olympic Games and the equestrian event in the Los Angeles Summer Olympics have reported temperature-related risks(HSE, 2012). The measures could include use of data to help assess risk, effective public information/announcements systems availability of hydration & drinking water, rescheduling events at appropriate times, provision of protection (such as sunscreen hats and portable shade canopies), and use of fans/heaters and Staff rotation etc(HSE, 2012) .

Respiratory Diseases

The site may be prone to air pollutants, such as dust, sulphur dioxide, aeroallergens, such as pollen etc that may cause respiratory problems to the people at the site. The measures to mitigate the risks could include water sprays for dust, the testing of seasonal allergens, public information systems and the availability of respiratory specialists.

Road Traffic Accident

Any major event attracts a lot of people to drive to the venue or the venue might be located in a busy traffic area. Such situations increase potential road accidents tend to increase during major events. Proper measures to reduce such incidents could include redirecting traffic, proper signage and volunteer supports, advising on traffic rules, seatbelt use and avoiding driving when tired etc (HSE, 2012).

Injuries to Public

There are often risks to the public due to slip and trip hazards, falls and traumatic injuries. For example during the 1996 Olympic Games in Atlanta, 30,000 people sought medical care with the most common incident being injury representing 30% of all cases (HSE, 2012). There is also a potential for the development of muscular-skeletal disorders (MSDs) due to excretive work by attests or workers. For example, during Sydney Games (2004), 326 street cleaners manually removed approximately 20 tonnes of rubbish from city streets, 5000kg of rubbish was removed from the Olympic Sites, city roadways were cleaned three times a day, 12 anti-graffiti cleaners worked around the clock for removing approximately 1300 instances of graffiti (HSE, 2012). Proper signage, information on public injuries, identification of potential points of hazards, support of mechanical equipment for cleaners, and ensuring medical preparedness, etc could be useful to avoid the risks(HSE, 2012).

Crowd Control

One of the major issues at any event is managing the movement of the crowd at entry, exits and in & around the venue. The excessive crowds in citation areas will put stress on resources and may lead to crashes and injuries. Incidents or fatalities involving crowds include 96 fatalities during Hillsborough events in 1989, 1426 fatalities during the Haj in Mecca in 1990, nine people were killed at the Roskilde rock concert in the year 2000(HSE, 2012). There can also be incidents involving smaller numbers that still have fatal results as was seen during a rush at the Ikea shop in Saudi Arabia Measures to mitigate and control crowds included: systems to manage crowds, safety announcements, Communication between staff, management by stewards and security staff with communication, blanking steward numbers based as per crowd size, crowd announcements, Design and planning using computer simulation, use of broadcast screens guide paths, ensuring staff are competent, considering groups such as the disabled, considering crowds beyond the venues(HSE, 2012)

The Strain on Health Care

Any events can have an impact on emergency planning and additional strain on health care and hospitals. For an instant, a 5.9% increase in ambulance calls was observed during the World Championship Games in Helsinki in 2005 and during the rugby world cup final held in Australia in 2003 (HSE, 2012). The proactive solutions could be public health response teams at the location, Provision of polyclinics for each subsite, transportation reach to emergency vehicles, coordination between authorities hospitals and police, adequate design – ensuring good site layout with clear access to emergency services etc (HSE, 2012).

Workplace Violence

public-facing job roles such as stewards, hospitality staff, health staff, sales, security staff, and taxi drivers are exposed to violence. The interventions could include, secure entry systems, violence audits, workplace inspections, presence of security guards and police, incident investigations and injury and illness records and public guidance and support systems(HSE, 2012).

Electricity and Fires, Carbon Monoxide etc.

The risk of fires at events could include structural fires and small-scale fires, such as litterbin fires and electric fires and shocks etc. for example; during the Sydney Olympics, the fire brigade responded to a total of 144 incidents and during the 2002 Salt Lake City Olympics the fire department faced challenges to access the incidents of fire (HSE, 2012). The proper fire risk assents systems, Pre-event inspections, hazards identification, and signage, Identifying and disposing of unexploded fireworks: fire exit signs and procedure, public announcement and guidance, Availability of resources and trained staff could be solutions for fire risk(HSE, 2012).

Food and Drinks Availability

Visibility of the right amount of safe and hygienic food and drinking facilities in appropriate numbers and at appropriate distances can avoid risks related to food and hygienic, diseases and crowd management.

Management of Health and Safety Risk and Emergency Plan

Managing a safe Event involves: Planning, Assessing risks, precautions measure and corrective and perverting actions, Contingency, and Emergency planning and procedures, effective communications, Managing crowd and resources, Review and reflection.The primary legislation covering occupational health and safety in Britain is the Health and Safety at Work Act 1974, which makes employers responsible for the management of health and safety. It sets out the general duties which employers have towards employees and members of the public, and employees have to themselves and to each other. This means taking reasonable steps to prevent harm coming to anyone involved in your event and forward planning in case of any emergency situations that could arise. The law is in place 'to ensure that risks to people's health and safety arising from work activities, including members of the public, self-employed persons, volunteers and contractors, are properly controlled'(HSE, 2000).

Two components of risk management are risk management strategies available(e.g. risk-informed, cautionary/ precautionary and discursive strategies) and; the structure of the risk management process(Aven, 2016).The risk-informed strategy aid in the treatment of risk – avoidance, reduction, transfer and retention – using risk assessments (Aven, 2016). The cautionary/precautionary strategy includes a plan for safety factors, reading signals or cues of risks, redundancy in safety devices, substitutes or diversified arrangements, containment, flexible response destines systems, immune system, and the improvement of conditions for emergency management and system adaptation (Aven, 2016). The discursive strategy includes action to build confidence and trustworthiness, through clarifications of facts, the involvement of affected people, reduction of uncertainties and ambiguities, deliberation and accountability (Aven, 2016).Risk management is often driven by policy and policy analysis. A policy can be defined as 'a set of rules, guides, principles or plans to guide decisions and achieve desirable outcomes for stakeholders, organisations, governments, and individuals' (Aven, 2016). The Cyclic process of policy development and analysis includes six phases such as; Problem identification; Generating alternatives, analysis; Processing for policy instruments development, consulting, deliberation and coordination; Decision-making; Implementation and Evaluation of the effectiveness of the policy (Aven, 2016).

The main principles of a H&S risk management policy are: Precautionary principle (including avoiding the event itself); Robustness (optimising resistance or self-protection, withstanding "vague approximations"); Resilience (flexible, adaptive, collective mindfulness, alertness, proactiveness with ability to sustain or restore its basic functionality following a stressor); Habits of High Reliability Organisations (preoccupation with failure, sensitivity to operations, reluctance to simplify, commitment to resilience and deference to expertise); principle of large/deep uncertainties (e.g. climate change and managing emerging disease); Principle of Surprises and black swans metaphor (Surprises do occur, think of Extremistan a world outside Mediocristan); Principle of risk acceptance criteria and tolerability criteria(risk constraints and evaluate their pros and cons, concerns, profits, safety, reputation, etc); The ALARP principle (ALARP: As Low As Reasonably Practicable- a risk-reduction principle, which is based on both risk-informed and cautionary/precautionary thinking of strategy and on cost benefit analysis);Principle of integrative thinking (balancing the tension being caused by the different perspectives and coordinating the whole framework of risk management) and Principle of Knowledge transfer and management (knowledge building, transfer of experience and learning, and adds theories and practical insight etc) and system thinking and continuous improvements son on (Aven, 2016).

The process of H&S risks management can be broken down into the number of steps, such as Set Purpose, goals and objectives of risk management activities; Use checklist to identify situations and events (hazards/threats/opportunities); Conduct cause and consequences analysis of these events, using techniques such as risk tree analysis; Judge the likelihood of the events and their consequences(consequences, probability and Knowledge, characteristics etc); Evaluate risk; Risk treatment and management ; implementations of Risk Management plans and actions (ISO 31000, Aven, 2016).

The next sections provide details on the process of H&S risk management.

Planning of Event

Good planning of events means for seeing, the events aim and objectives, and putting in place process, procedure, actors, and resources for useful execution of the event as well as planning for mitigating any kind of health and safety risks. It needs engagement with various actors, agencies and resources. The risks such as due to overcrowding as well due to routine operations such as fire, trip hazards, electricity wire, fights or unexpected attacks or natural calamity should be foreseen and planned for.

To manage event risk it's essential to focus on goals and safety — not just compliance. Effective risk management minimizes potential costs and liabilities and leads to safer, more enjoyable events. Event planners should develop a risk management plan to effectively manage risks that might impact on an event. The plan should outline all of the steps, policies, and procedures that you are taking to mitigate risks. Establishing an appropriate and effective governance framework should be your first priority when designing an operating model for the delivery of an event. Early investment in proper governance structures and processes will result in more effective decision-making, risk management and outcomes. Understanding the distinction between "governance" and "management and operations" is particularly important in the context of events:

- **Governance (the board):** is responsible for determining the organisational purpose, vision, strategy and values — that is, where the organisation is heading and how it will get there
- **Management and Operations:** Are responsible for undertaking the activities required to achieve the goals and objectives set by the board. The aim is to identify potential hazards in your event and take the necessary steps to protect yourself and others.
- **Capacity:** Can your attendees be safely accommodated inside the venue? Will they be standing or seated? Is there room to circulate? Are there pinch points where overcrowding could occur?
- **Access:** Is there sufficient access to the event site/venue for pedestrians and vehicles? Are people with disabilities, wheelchairs or pushchairs able to access the venue? Are there enough emergency exits?
- **Hazards:** Does the site have any existing hazards, such as overhead electric powerlines or buried services that your structures could interfere with? Is it prone to flooding or high winds? Consider ground conditions and topography when positioning any temporary structures.
- **Facilities:** How far away are the nearest hospital and fire stations? What are the public transport links like? Consider the infrastructure you need for your event.

Health and safety should consider a range of stakeholders' points of view:

1. Event organiser
2. Site/venue owner
3. Contractor
4. Supervisor/worker
5. Volunteer
6. Local Licensing / authorising the authority

Assessing Risks

The risk easements ‘ involves the identification and assessment of risks to crowd safety within a venue and the development of steps required to minimise them ‘ (HSE, 2000). Depending upon the outcome of the risk assessment the event paneers have to follow a systematic process to identify potential hazards that could affect crowd safety, e.g. estimate the size of the problems, surging and swaying, and decide what you need to do to address the problems.

Health and safety of events should also Carry out a risk assessment and addressee the following:

1. Venue and site design
2. Temporary demountable structures
3. Managing crowds safely
4. Using barriers at events
5. Transport
6. Trip or equipment risks
7. Falls from height
8. Electrical safety
9. Fire safety
10. Crowd management risks
11. Crew Hazards
12. Weather and environment risks
13. Catering risks
14. Child and Vulnerable people protection,
15. Special effects
16. Noise
17. Amusements and attractions
18. Employee welfare
19. Handling waste

The planers should clearly write and communicate a different kind of potentialize hazard and corresponding corrective and preventive measures that need to be taken care of by the planers, actors and event attendees. These could include safety signs, symbols, safety routes and hazards potential areas and corresponding actions.

Contingency and Emergency Planning and Procedures

The planers should be ready for unexpected risks and hazards such as overcrowding, fall of event stalls, fire, terrorist attacks, heavy rains, or other unexpected risks.

Develop emergency procedures to be followed by anyone working on the event and discuss your plans with the venue management.

Aspects to consider when developing procedures include:

- **Raising the Alarm:** How will you communicate the emergency with staff and volunteers?
- **Informing the Public:** Do you have an adequate public address system? What is the procedure for stopping (and restarting) the show?
- **Onsite Emergency Response:** Are there fire extinguishers? Do you need security staff?
- **Summoning and Liaising With the Emergency Services:** Who will be your point of contact and how will you assist the emergency services?
- **Crowd Management (Including Evacuation):** How will you move people away from immediate danger to a place of safety? Don't forget to take people with limited mobility and children into consideration.
- **Traffic Management:** How will emergency vehicles gain access to the site? How will vehicles leave the site in the event of an emergency?
- **Providing First Aid**: Are their sufficient medical provisions?
- **Handling Casualties:** How will patients be taken to a hospital? Will there be ambulances onsite?

Monitoring the crowd and Implementing health and safety

It is important that the event organisers have kept in place a range of procedures and processes of movements of crowds and measures in order to address the impacts of such movements of crowds. Also, the event organise are responsible for managing your staff, suppliers and attendees to ensure they are not exposed to risk at all the different phases of the event, from set-up to break down.The organisers should provide staff with relevant information during the site induction and ensure suppliers do the same for their employees. This should include information such as site hazards, speed limits and parking, first aid, toilets, and wash facilities, and emergency arrangements. You may also want to provide relevant health and safety information to the public in the form of signage and/or a pre-event announcement. It is very important theta the event organisers continually monitor risks throughout your event by creating a checklist and having a nominated individual/s responsible for checking at regular intervals. A clear and competently implemented paper trail is the best way for event organisers to mitigate risk.

So far as is Reasonably Practicable' (SFAIRP) Model of Risk Management

A person or organisation that creates risk is required to manage and control that risk so that it is reduced 'So Far As Is Reasonably Practicable' (SFAIRP) through design, management and procedural measures (Russ, 2010). In 1970, Robens Report recommended 'the unification within a single comprehensive framework of legal action of the main Statutes bearing on safety and health at work, thus giving rise to Health and Safety at Work Act 1974 and the creation of the Health and Safety Executive (HSE) (Russ, 2010). The act stipulated a range of H&S responsibilities to employers, designers, manufacturers, suppliers, and other stakeholders. In summary, the Act requires employers to develop H&S policy, assess risks, corrective and preventive plans and so on. The system could include plaining on - What could go wrong and Hazards? How bad could it be to plant, people, the planet? What is already being done to minimise the risk? What new actions are required to further reduce the risk? Review and update? (Russ, 2010). The risks assessors can create risk matrix and risk tree or graph; which will identify the kind of risks during activities during the whole process, along with the probability and consequence in form of the number of adverse impacts, etc and the actions required to ensure risk is reduced SFAIRP.

The next section discusses some case studies to illustrate the improper or incomplete usage of the SFAIRP model.

Case Study 1: Dream space (2006):

Dreamspace was a large inflatable structure (50X50X5 M), inside which members of the public could walk around to experience a dream-like world of light and sound. He structures lifted up to a near-vertical position resulting in 2 Fatalities, 27 Injured (Russ, 2010). HSE prosecuted all parties, the Designer, the Contract Company and the Public Park Authority, for failing to protect the health and safety.

Case Study 2: ICL Plastics a factory in Glasgow, UK.

An explosion happened in 2004 due to underground LPG pipe leakage, that demolished the building killing 9 workers and injuring 33(Russ, 2010).It could have been prevented by following the SFAIRP model.

Case Study 3 The Kumbh Mela (India):

The Kumbh Mela is a religious event in India that constitutes the largest number of people gathered (120 million visitors in 2013) at a specific place and at a specific time. It is older than the Hajj and many other religious, political, cultural, music and sports events (David & Roy, 2016). Mass gathering events pose critical health challenges, especially for the control of the disease. Citing World Health Organization (WHO), (David & Roy, 2016) stated that a mass gathering is 'any occasion, either organized or spontaneous, that attracts sufficient numbers of people to strain the planning and response resources of the community, city or nation hosting the event'. An event of such a mass gathering poses a unique set of public health challenges, including stampedes, crush injuries, burns due to fires, exposure to extreme weather, infectious diseases, water-, sanitation-, and hygiene-related illnesses, and epidemic outbreaks (David & Roy, 2016). Thus it needs plans for disease surveillance, infection control, and water and sanitation, etc.

The name Kumbh Mela etiologically means urn -fair (Kumbha- Mela). The religious-cultural event's roots back to a legendary battle between the gods and demons in Hindu mythology for the elixir of life by churning the primordial ocean of life. The fight for the elixir led to accidentally tiling the urn of elixir and four drops to fall on the four cities of Allahabad, Nashik, Ujjain, and Haridwar, where the Kumbh Mela is held (David & Roy, 2016). Thus each city Allahabad, Nashik, Ujjain, and Haridwar hosts the event every 12 years on the dates pre-determined based on special combinations of the zodiac. The events are organized on the banks of the rivers in each of the four cities, the main tradition associated with the Kumbh Mela is ritual bathing in the river on certain auspicious days during the 3-month period of the festival. In such a Mass gathering (s, the number of devotees attending the Kumbh Mela has increased logarithmically, from around 400 000 in 1903 to 120 million in 2013) occasions the potential for health and safety risks are huge. Kumbh Mela involves temporary human settlement, a 'pop-up city' of the canvas, corrugated metal sheets, bamboo, nails, and rope in the flood plains of the rivers, which houses and feeds millions of people for 3 months every year 3 years(David & Roy, 2016). Unlike other places of religious, cultural or sports events, the monitoring of a number of visitors at Kumbh Mela is not possible due to people's unplanned visits and open entry and exits areas. There were sporadic epidemics during the Kumbh Mela in 1892, 1948, and in the 1960s. also in 1954 Kumbh Mela, a stampede killed nearly 500 people and injured around 2000 (David & Roy, 2016). This led to the enquiry commission and led to the rather effective planning and organization of the Kumbh Mela by better coordination among stakeholders and self-regulation by the visitors.

Whereas in 1966 there was just a single 100- bed temporary hospital; in contrast, in 2013 the government ensured a hospital in each of the 14 zones of the Kumbh Mela area of 1936 hectares, 24 alternative medicine hospitals (such as Ayurveda and homeopathy) and 150 first aid posts staffed by a doctor and a pharmacist, as well as 120 ambulance and a central hospital and, a telemedicine centre at the main field hospital of the Kumbh Mela, which collected daily information on the inpatient and outpatient cases reported and a a mobile telemedicine unit for video-conferencing and to conduct minor surgeries (David & Roy, 2016). Given the history of waiter borne diseases (cholera, diarrhea etc) the government has focussed on compulsory inoculation, availability of potable water, sanitation, and hygiene in minimizing health risks, rapid monitoring, and prompt public health interventions. For an instant, in the year 2013, forty-six protected bore wells with chlorination attached tanks, as well piped potable water through 20 000 taps and 35 000 toilets were constructed in the Kumbh Mela area. The case clearly illustrates that the process of event management with an integrated and coordinated approach can lead to the effective management of health and safety at events of mass guttering.

Case 4: Glastonbury Festival And Other 'Greenfield' Music Festivals:

The Glastonbury Festival of Contemporary Performing Arts is one of the largest greenfield festivals in the world running over five days with approximately 175,000 visitors and staff on the 900-acre site, a large temporary city that has the potential of huge risks to public safety. However, an effective stem of event planning, risk assents, coordination, communication, control=l, and management has led to the effective management of such festive in in the UK.

Health & Safety, National Systems, Culture and Role of Volunteer

Different countries have adopted alternative systems for managing events of large scale.

Chinese State Council executive passed "large-scale mass activities, safety regulations" to ensure effective management of events. This regulation requires event organizers to repose the activities and specific implementation of security, while the governmental body supervises the safety work. The relations balance between risks and benefits, between the rights and obligations etc. In china attention is paid to central law and regulations, coordination among members of professional Governmental Management Team drawn from Police, Traffic, Fire-protection, and Military and event organisers etc; developing an effective Risk management and control system of events ; Raising risk awareness and building a climate a culture of risk assessment, estimation and management (Shangjun & Xinjian, 2012).

In Germany, H&S risk management at large events include provisions for Professional Police for big events, standardize private security and insurance system, pay attention to intelligence analysis, establish pre-warning assessment systems, and corrective and preventive systems (Shangjun & Xinjian, 2012).In Japan, the system includes a professional & private security system, crowd control strategy, strict countermeasures and panned security projects (Shangjun & Xinjian, 2012). In the USA, H&S systems include; Investigation Systems, Patrol & monitoring systems, highly developed private security systems and using high tech Technogym for security (Shangjun & Xinjian, 2012).

Safety culture is those parts of the organizational culture that influence values, attitudes, and behaviors towards health and safety in the organization (Nielsen, 2014). Organizational culture is defined as 'a pattern of shared basic assumptions (unconscious, taken-for-granted beliefs that are the ultimate source of values and actions) that a group has learned as it solved issues of external adaptation and internal integration' (Schein, 2004 cited in Nielsen, 2014). The shared assumption is taken for granted, implicit theories-in-use, artefacts (visible organizational structures and processes that are easy to observe but hard to decipher) and beliefs and values (strategies, goals and philosophies that serve as the espoused justifications for actions theories') all agreed rights and wrongs that guide individual behaviours (Argyris & Schön, 1996 cited by Nielsen, 2014). organizational culture can be changed intentionally and 'it serves as an anxiety-reducing function, as it gives people a frame of reference for how to act, think, and feel in new situations, and a learned defines mechanism against uncertainty and change' (Nielsen, 2014).

As per the cultural iceberg principle, the organizational culture can not be fully seen or measured, however, it can be observed through artefacts, and organizational climate of shared perceptions of organizational policies, practices, and procedures, both formal and informal. Thus organisations and event organisations should use artefacts and organisational climate for safety so as to change safety culture at an organisation. As organizational culture serves as an anxiety-reducing function for people to act, think, and feel, thus any attempt to change culture will bring in new threats and anxieties to the people.

A safety climate is formed by the workers' perception of the relative priority of safety versus efficiency goals (Zohar, 2000 cited in Nielsen, 2014). The number of dimensions of safety climate include management commitment, supervisor competence, the priority of safety overproduction, and time pressure (Flin et al., 2000 in Mearns, Whitaker, & Flin, 2003). Safety management relates to the *actual* practices, roles and functions associated with remaining safe (Mearns et al., 2003). The climate is created by supervisors and leaders' behaviours, daily communications, and practices and in particular their commitments to health and safety. Transformational leaders are charismatic, inspiring, stimulating, and considerate. Transformational leaders provide followers with a sense of purpose; portray an image of success, self-confidence, and self-belief; articulate shared goals, mutual understanding, and an attractive future (Flin & Yule, 2004). The leadership practices, attitude, behaviours and communications are influenced not only by their own values but also due to organisational systems, policies as well as external pressures from stakeholders and organisational and national health and safety organization (HSO) or committee (HSC) and international H&S organisations. Thus the creation of H&S climate and culture requires multidimensional actions from both internal and external forces.

The events not only utilize permanent paid employees but also takes help from a number of volunteers. Volunteering has been defined as 'any activity in which time is given freely to benefit another person, group, or organisation' (Wilson 2000). The volunteer is the people who volunteer to help at events. As the size of events, significance and costs increase the need for volunteering is further increased. For example during the 2012 Olympic in London used 70,000 volunteers and World Cup in Russia (2018) a total of 17,000 volunteers were selected from a pool of 170,000 applicants (Etchells 2018); similarly during World Cup in Brazil (2014), 15,000 volunteers were deployed and it is estimated that in 2022 World Cup in Qatar, around 16,000 volunteers will be required(Strang, 2018). public-facing roles can involve volunteers directing fans to correct locations, supervising queues, welcoming fans to stadiums and answering questions about the event, checking tickets, and undertaking many other responsibilities (Strang, 2018). The motivation to volunteering include pride in their community and their country, social enrichment by engaging with others, sense of personal satisfaction, to gain experience, skills development opportunities, a passion for sport/music/culture, experience that was different from their everyday life, wellbeing of volunteers, public and individual recognition etc. AS volunteer is present at key points of potential health and safety risks, it is paramount that there is an effective system for Selection of volunteers, Training, maintaining motivation, preventing attrition: caring for the wellbeing of volunteers; attempting to match volunteers to roles that suit their interests and abilities; managing the expectations of volunteers; communicating clearly and consistently; and recognizing the efforts (Strang, 2018). Further creating, communicating and implementing a climate of health and safety through volunteer is very important.

Managerial Implications and Scope for Future Research

The chapter details and guides managers to consider national culture, organization culture, organisational climate, risk management climate, risk management systems, procedures, principles and process in order to manage larger events successively and effectively without any potential tragedies, harms and risks. Further research can be carried out to undertake a systematic literature review on risk management practices and processes in different countries and cultures and develop a comprehensive actionable model for managing, minimizing and mitigating negative consequences of risk associated with organising small and big events.

CONCLUSION

An event involves organisation a project that involves a range of activities, actors, subbasements and procedures and processes. The event organising involves managing health and safety risks. The Risks should be monitored as managed as per the law of land and the viewpoint of various stakeholders should be considered for the successful implementation of risk at an event. The organising involved in event management can make use of organisation culture, organizational climate, organisational policy, HSO policies, and national and international body regulations and guidelines in order to effectively manages health and safety risks at events.

REFERENCES

Aven, T. (2016, August 16). Risk assessment and risk management: Review of recent advances on their foundation. *European Journal of Operational Research*, *253*(1), 1–13. doi:10.1016/j.ejor.2015.12.023

David, S., & Roy, N. (2016). Public health perspectives from the biggest human mass gathering on earth: Kumbh Mela, India. *International Journal of Infectious Diseases*, *47*, 42–45. doi:10.1016/j.ijid.2016.01.010 PMID:26827807

Flin, R., & Yule, S. (2004). Leadership for safety: Industrial experience. *Quality & Safety in Health Care*, *13*(suppl_2), 45–51. doi:10.1136/qshc.2003.009555 PMID:15576692

HSE. (2000). *Managing crowds safely, A guide for organisers at events and venues*. HSE Books.

HSE. (2012). *RR811 - A literature review of the health and safety risks associated with major sporting events - Learning lessons for the London 2012 Olympic and Paralympic games*. Retrieved from http://www.hse.gov.uk/research/rrpdf/rr811.pdf

Levy, R., Bogin, B., Gretz, S., Aharonov, R., & Slonim, N. (2018). *Towards an argumentative content search engine using weak supervision*. Academic Press.

Mearns, K., Whitaker, S. M., & Flin, R. (2003). Safety climate, safety management practice and safety performance in offshore environments. *Safety Science*, *41*(8), 641–680. doi:10.1016/S0925-7535(02)00011-5

Nielsen, K. J. (2014). Improving safety culture through the health and safety organization: A case study. *Journal of Safety Research*, *48*, 7–17. doi:10.1016/j.jsr.2013.10.003 PMID:24529086

Reid, S., & Ritchie, B. (2011). Risk management: Event managers' attitudes, beliefs, and perceived constraints. *Event Management*, *15*(4), 329–341. doi:10.3727/152599511X13175676722528

Russ, K. (2010). Risk assessment in the UK health and safety system: Theory and practice. *Safety and Health at Work*, *1*(1), 11–18. doi:10.5491/SHAW.2010.1.1.11 PMID:22953158

Shangjun, W., & Xinjian, Z. (2012). Problems of Mega-events Engineering Risk Management in China. *Systems Engineering Procedia*, *4*, 431–437. doi:10.1016/j.sepro.2012.01.007

Strang, L. (2018). *Insights on the role of volunteers in public safety at major sporting events Case study*. Retrieved from www.randeurope.org

The Event Brite. (2018). *Guide to health and safety*. Retrieved from https://www.eventbrite.co.uk/blog/guide-health-and-safety-for-events-ds00/

Chapter 3
Event Management

Bilan Sahidi
The University of Sunderland, UK

ABSTRACT

In this chapter, the sustainability and development related to corporate social responsibility is assessed. The intermediate approaches of group thinking and their future possibilities are discussed in brief. It will be helpful to break the orthodox mentality and also for future purpose to bring development and innovation in the society. The techniques of current approaches regarding the thinking process and their impact on the society are assessed. The group thinking has been assessed through a particular mentality of the society. The process of implementing change in the recent mentality and the platform to implement the process has been analyzed in the context of learning and development.

INTRODUCTION

The sustainability and development related to CSR have been disusing in terms of a particular event in the country, it has been signified through the precious and current context compaction. Accordant to the observation, current conditions related to the Tackling Groupthink & Orthodoxy in Sustainability have been discussed in relation to the Corporate Social Responsibility. In this study, the current conditions related to the group thinking as well as the present condition of groupthink and orthodoxy in sustainability have been described in an elaborate manner. Also, the role of implementing the Groupthink activities has also been mentioned in the study.

DOI: 10.4018/978-1-7998-3230-0.ch003

Overview of the Event

The event of **Tackling Groupthink & Orthodoxy in Sustainability** took place in February of 2019. It is a recent event which focused on maintaining the groupthink and its impact in the country is related to corporate social responsibility. The group thinking and its implementation in real life are related to resolving the main problems of today's society in the UK. Previous thinking mechanism in terms of daily operation was successful for that particular period of the community. Millen Baker, an unknown CSR commentator and podcaster has delivered a speech on the development of group thinking and orthodox mentality tackling.

He has the experience of delivering different speeches in a different context that has helped to change the thinking process of a particular country. The speaker demonstrated the main reason for the orthodox mentality and thus implementing various procedures for diminishing this kind of mental obligations. The reason for sticking to the one-way process of thinking includes climate change and the lifestyles of the particular region. The institution Academia has consigned some of the practical solutions that helped identify the main reason for being stuck at the same mentality for more timespan (Scherer *et al.* 2016).

The particular aspect of changing lifestyle and brief understanding as per the speaker has been demonstrated due to the group or community-based habit. In order to correct the orthodox mentality, continuous change and learning might be needed. In the current aspect, the learning mentality is stagnant, and thus it is very difficult for the people to make their mind work accordingly to the current tradition of the thinking process. The event has been arranged with the help of UK volunteers who were attached with the governmental help and also by the help of different private agencies that provide manpower through the event of Tackling Groupthink & Orthodoxy in Sustainability.

In order to accommodate the huge number of people, there were more space and accommodation has been arranged in the meeting. The event of Tackling Groupthink & Orthodoxy in Sustainability has risen the funding from the government as well as the private institute who were associated with different NGOs. A specific time frame was implemented for wider participation. The intelligence and thinking process is related to the success of the message that has been delivered in the seminar. It could be helpful for the countrymen in the future time frame. Due to the suggestion that has been delivered for the improvement of thinking, it became easy for the people of a particular country to make their daily life simpler (Martínez, Fernandez and Fernández, 2016).

The Objective of Event

The objective of the event is described below

- To make the people aware of the current thinking process through the event of Tackling Groupthink & Orthodoxy in Sustainability.
- To implement the new thinking process a part of daily life.
- To have less complexity in group thinking in life through the event of Tackling Groupthink & Orthodoxy in Sustainability.
- To reduce the orthodox mentality in the life of UK citizens.
- To maintain the corporate social responsibility in the particular process.

The Current Condition of Groupthink & Orthodoxy in Sustainability Related to CSR

According to the surrounding and the nature of any business helped to determine the sustainability, context of orthodox and group thinking, sustainability in a particular country. The social terms, as well as the environment terms of that business, will help to make it cost much lower than any unsustainable business in the country. The broader frameworks in terms of the interrelation of the corporate social responsibility will help get risks management and other strategies implemented in the right way. The complex relationship with the group of the internal assessment and other sections of the company has been known to get the consistency reduced. In order to make the improvement of the management, it has been seen that very bright and meaningful economic reality must have to be implemented in the company. In order to ensure the sustainability achieved within a particular time, building and cultivating good relations with the employees and stakeholders is essential. The internal and external assessment would not be done due to the lacking in growth approach in those particular agents. In order to transform and develop any business, the context of good culture and development through learning is equally important as money.

There are some of the things in terms of sustainability that is beneficial for a business to develop for the future.

- Identification and creation of long term value related to organization growth by the event of Tackling Groupthink & Orthodoxy in Sustainability.
- Effective economic, social and environmental risk management for better corporate social responsibility by Tackling Groupthink & Orthodoxy in Sustainability.
- Loyalty and trust-building for the customers due to the services and product delivery.

- Reduction of operating cost due to effective resource and supply management.

The orthodox mentality, in terms of lifestyle and future maintenance, has been maintained. Among most of the significance in sustainability and corporate responsibility has been comprehended. The current mentality is abed on learning and progression rather than being stuck at the previous concept. In context to the implementation of making more development in the area of each and every activity, it is extremely important to track current progress and in accordance with those weakest sectors could be easily identified, for example, looking and preserving vulnerable people in a safe house.

There are several tasks such as activities related to sports and studies as well as to take participation in the social gathering, which could improve the corporate social responsibility. It will also help in improving the cognitive ability of the particular thinking of the people in terms of achieving quick results in each sector. For example, a care worker must ensure safety of vulnerable people who live roadside.

Embracing the growth of each sector and their maintenance progress is really appreciable. It will help in getting better and to the point-based approaches so that they could be utilized shortly. The sustainability report in every year must be published so that in terms of the previous year, the growth of the current year has been taken into consideration.

The particular assessment in different studies and its relation with the particular project has to be admired that could give an edge to people for developing mindset. In order to make the thinking process done, longer period of time is spent on creative things, which includes painting and writing, reading of different types of stories, for example, road accidents, death by extreme cold or numina.

The improvement in thinking approach will also help in the imagination power of the people. The group thinking abilities such as the correct decision making and implementing the techniques of a blueprint is being improved through better collaboration through online and offline process. The group development of any particular project will be achieved with the help of a particular leadership and its followers to be on track. In the competition with the other events, the current aspect of maintaining sustainable development will be helpful for the event.

The responsibility of stakeholders and its engagement in daily activities are the main reason to growth company to the topmost position in the particular sector. The particular aspect of growing and maintaining the current company is needed to have a sustainable competition to develop their mindset. The social responsibility also includes high perception of growth and relevance in the context. The high performance and its relevant aspiration must adhere to the company upper management that could help in engaging actions to be taken (Cui *et al.* 2018).

Previous Condition of Groupthink and Orthodoxy in Sustainability-Related to CSR in UK

In the early condition of the country, it has been seen that most of the Orthodox based relation is sustained through the old mentality based people. They were stuck to the precious old way and not based not interested in the recent ways which hold more efficient rather than previous ones. The Precious method of doing things likes daily operation, and the other activities are based on the lengthy and very time-consuming process. The precious mentality of thinking and considering different facts which were not particular in the context of solving problems, most of the unworthy and very difficult process has been mentioned (Voegtlin and Greenwood,2016).

The problem-solving approach and different types of disregarding approach has been configured through the better approaches are much time-consuming. The better growth and sustainability of previous thinking is based on non-growth mentality, Growth and responsibility have these future scope related to the work-based comprehension. The process of completing the necessary health events like blood donation camp and its future based aspect is needed to have consisted of better management through high performance in the representative perspective (Cronqvist and Yu, 2015).

The thinking was based on a single pattern that was applicable to all of the problems which were not correct. In the perspective of this approach, there are some of the aspects that are being concerned through guidance and expert opinion. This expert opinion and guidance of the proper perception are related to the emergency blood donation campaign and thus risks exposure was not high in the context. The best possible aspects are needed to be improved and maintained through the utmost coverage of stronger aspect.

The previous mentality of orthodox activities is not that helpful in terms of the development and improvement of mental growth. The learning and development mentality was not much improved in context to the comparison of current comparison. The mentality of solving the blood lose problems in a particular way is based on having the direct approach of blood donation camp as CSR event, and its relevant prospect is to be collected through direct and indirect management. The current prospect of gaining more of internal approaches, such as defining the current problem and improving the current method has never been examined. It would be very difficult in terms of the growth and development based learning objective. The group thinking in terms of proper context was not resolved through the internal assessment.

In order to grow more contextual segments in the approach of learning and development, there should be accurate to the context management based approaches which are needed to be mentioned. The prospect of blood donation campaign development and its relevant approaches might be helpful for better assessment through the internal approaches.

The reasoning was busily propounded on a solitary example that was pertinent for the majority of the issues which was not in the least right. In the viewpoint of this methodology, some of the viewpoints are being worried through the direction and master supposition. The master assessment and direction of the best possible discernment is identified with the crisis the approaches along with these hazardous activities which might be high in the specific situation.

The ideal perspectives should have been improved and kept according to the inclusion of the very own perspective. The past mindset of conventional kind of activities like blood donation camp is not that helpful as far as the advancement and improvement of mental development. The learning and development are not much improved in setting to the examination of current correlation. The mindset of taking care of the health issues of vulnerable people in society with a certain goal in mind depends on having the immediate methodology of correspondence (Campopiano and De Massis, 2015).

It is a pertinent prospect to be gathered through the immediate and backhanded administration. The present prospect of increasing a higher context of interior methodologies, for example, characterizing the present issue and improving the present technique has never been analyzed. It would be extremely troublesome as far as the development and advancement based learning objective. The gathering thinking regarding legitimate setting was not settled through the inside assessment. The possibility of advancement and its important methodologies may be useful for better evaluation through the interior approaches.

Comparison of Current and Previous Condition

In terms of the comparison to the current and previous condition, it has been specified that much improvement in the context of the structure of CSR thinking and its significance prospect has been taken into consideration. The higher context of managing the thinking process has been approached through very better consequences, for example, free health checkup centers. The current context has been maintained through the proper problem finding and its maintenance to be concurrently signified in the time and cost-saving method. The previous group thinking was not specifically been done in context, improves to make the health monitoring process easily doable.

In the current framework, there are several changes those should be implemented through a particular description. The high quality of improvement and its perfect implementation through a particular aspect, there are some of the reasons which were not that particular in the context of better implementation of the better aspects.

The better development of getting new things to be customized according to the facts the future development based activities are being taken into consideration.

The Improvement of having much consideration in the relevant thinking process, the current approaches must have to be arranged accordingly that step by step achievement is easily done. The interested approaches of making the signified approach in the heavy and accumulative aspect are made in the newer context that is based on having success achieved in the little span of time. In order to make the collaboration with the time and cost, it has been estimated that more current context of growth and development has been maintained. The flexibility of design thinking and cognitive ability has not been implemented in a previous way. In a current way, the flexibility of learning and development has very indulged comprehension. The better approaches such as examining the current growth of the company and making the respective changes in the company are needed to be implemented in the particular approaches.

According to the comparison, it could be stated that most of the internal assessment in assessing daily life activities have been done in recent days, which will help in solving the recent activity based problem in an easier way. The better progress of assessment in the context of achieving them significant assessment has been very easily modified. It would give freedom to make the flexibility of thinking, and thus orthodox mentality has been changed .the higher context of implementing a little bit of urgency in any typical thing has been taken care in the recent days which has not been contested in the previous days.

As far as the correlation with the present and past consideration, it has been indicated that much improvement with regards to the structure of reasoning and its prospect has been thought about. The higher setting of the thinking process has been drawn closer through extremely better outcomes. The present setting has kept up through the correct issue and its as simultaneously meant in the time and cost sparing technique. The past gathering believing was not explicitly been done in setting improves to make the procedure effectively possible.

It was then seen as the most reasonable for that time as it were. In the present time, there are a few changes that should have been actualized through the specific depiction. The high calibre of progress and its ideal execution through a specific angle, there is a portion of the reasons which were not excessively specific in setting of better usage of the better perspectives. The better improvement of getting the new things to be modified by the realities the future advancement based exercises are being thought about.

The Improvement of having much thought in the applicable reasoning procedure, the present methodologies must be masterminded as needs be that bit by bit accomplishment is effectively done. The intrigued methodologies of making the implied methodology in the substantial and collective angle are done in the more up to date setting that depends on having achievements accomplished in the little range of time. So as to make a cooperation with the time and cost, it has been evaluated that increasingly present setting of development and advancement has been kept up.

The adaptability of configuration thinking and subjective capacity has not been executed in a past way. In a present way, the adaptability of learning and improvement has very enjoyed perception. Through this, a greater amount of the simultaneous methodologies has been dealt with, which will like the assistance to be depended to make the corporate social duty generally excellent. The better methodologies, for example, looking at the present development of the organization and rolling out the separate improvements in the organization should have been actualized in the specific approaches like self-development and self-actualization.

Role of Implementing Groupthink in Academia

As per the current approach of improvement, group thinking has been improved to maintain corporate social activities. The context of maintaining integrity in the thorough process, the background of the current thinking as well as the future thinking has been changed. In order to make the implementation more approachable and more positive, some of the expert guidance has been taken in order to make the improvement realistic and to the point. The context of implementing the thinking and strategy changes, there are some of the aspects such as high quality of authentication and its premature configuration with the relevant prospect have been implemented. The approach of making more actions done in less time, the quickest method has been taken into consideration (Benlemlih and Bitar, 2018).

The corporate social responsibility in terms of the current approaches of group thinking and its recent traditions has been comprehended through the final plan and its utilization to be processed. The higher approach of maintaining the responsibility towards the society has been taken into care through the help which has been provided in the recent tradition of thinking. The higher quality of maintenance and its perfect assessment have been managed within the context. The internal assessment of the thinking technique and its related approaches have been taken into consideration.

Recommendations for Improvement

In order to improve more in a particular topic, there are some approaches that might be taken in context to the precious mistakes to be avoided. The main fundamentals, such as the process could be modified and maintained as per the current flexibility of approach in the thinking perspectives. The previous note flexible methods must be abolished through the better context of simple, marketing and management based works in the progressive approaches.

The corporate social responsibility needs more of the environment-friendly human behaviour based vacation. These actions are included but not limited to make more trees implemented, fewer vehicles to commute on the road and less pollution to be released in the air regarding the industrial and non-industrial approaches. These approaches will make sure that in the context of having better approaches of corporate social responsibility, the improvement of better concept and more approaches are needed to be improved in the recent context. The recommended approaches are also based on having better approaches, such as the responsibility of not spreading any rumours of any typical concepts to be signified in or outside the office premises.

The improvement of effective assessment in the corporate social responsibility is increasing the awareness of the ecological basis of assumption. The very best approaches related to learning and development will be helpful in future progress. The approaches related to making growth and development are based on guidance through the betterment of approaches is needed to be done.

The context and development of making the orthodox mentality to be redesigned, more approach in the thinking innovation has to be mentioned in the current context of design thinking. The past non-adaptable techniques must be cancelled through the better set of simple, marketing and executives based works in the progressive methodologies. The corporate social duty needs a greater amount of nature cordial human conduct based vacation.

These activities are incorporated, however not restricted to make greener environment actualized, fewer vehicles to drive out and about and less contamination to be discharged noticeable all around with respect to the mechanical and non-modern approaches. These methodologies will ensure that with regards to having the better methodologies of corporate social obligation, the improvement of a better idea and more methodologies should have been improved in the ongoing setting. The suggested methodologies are additionally founded on having better methodologies, for example, the duty of not spreading any gossip to be implied in or outside the workplace premises.

The improvement of compelling evaluation in the corporate social responsibility is regarded in expanding the familiarity with the earth premise of supposition. The absolute methodologies identified with the learning and advancement will be useful later on advancement. Definitive methodologies identified with make development and advancement depend on the direction through the improvement of methodologies should have been finished.

Future Scope

It can be assumed that in the future time frame, the management bodies and the other growing corporate bodies have been focusing on the Corporate Social Responsibility for challenging the core orthodoxy. It can be assessed that the Corporate Social Responsibility is one of the crucial platforms that will get polarized in between the opponents and proponents, which has been transformed over the last twenty years.

The transformation has been much important and frowned upon ideas have also been evolving. Those are related to the orthodox behaviours of human beings, and it controls their attitudes within the business world. On the other hand, it can be noticed that the organizations will also treat the orthodoxy with safe hands and will be factorized with caution by exploring the key concepts to the open researchers. In this manner, the researchers will be able to elaborate on the capabilities and thus scrutinizing the key roles of Corporate Social Responsibility along with its implications.It can be noted that in the future scope, the representation of encounters within the local communities and global enterprises will be much prominent. In the present scenario of Corporate Social Responsibility, It can be observed that substantial progress is also necessary. Thus, due to this reason, the protests against the Macron and the fuel duty will also decrease within the limited time frame.

The Paris Agreement is also much useful, and the impact should also be reduced from the current state. In addition, the global enterprises existing within the global energy market will become more attractive and will create diverse extractive hot zones. Thus, in this manner, the fertile grounds will help for more government innovations. The sites will also get converted into more useful one, and the researchers can practice emerging government practices at the same point of time.

CONCLUSION

It can be concluded that Tackling Groupthink & Orthodoxy in Sustainability is one of the important events which takes place in the month of February 2019. It is a useful event that helped to increase the thinking capabilities by removing the previous thinking mechanisms at the same time frame. On the other hand, in this study, the main objectives of the event have also been described, which includes making people aware and thus implementing raw thinking procedures in the daily life of human beings. At the same time, having less complexity in the group thinking is very useful, and that has been implemented with the help of Tackling Groupthink & Orthodoxy in Sustainability.

REFERENCES

Benlemlih, M., & Bitar, M. (2018). Corporate social responsibility and investment efficiency. *Journal of Business Ethics, 148*(3), 647–671. doi:10.100710551-016-3020-2

Campopiano, G., & De Massis, A. (2015). Corporate social responsibility reporting: A content analysis in family and non-family firms. *Journal of Business Ethics, 129*(3), 511–534.

Martínez, J. B., Fernández, M. L., & Fernández, P. M. R. (2016). Corporate social responsibility: Evolution through institutional and stakeholder perspectives. *European Journal of Management and Business Economics*, *25*(1), 8–14.

Cronqvist, H., & Yu, F. (2017). Shaped by their daughters: Executives, female socialization, and corporate social responsibility. *Journal of Financial Economics, 126*(3), 543–562. doi:10.1016/j.jfineco.2017.09.003

Cui, J., Jo, H., & Na, H. (2018). Does corporate social responsibility affect information asymmetry? *Journal of Business Ethics, 148*(3), 549–572. doi:10.100710551-015-3003-8

De Villiers, C., & Marques, A. (2016). Corporate social responsibility, country-level predispositions, and the consequences of choosing a level of disclosure. *Accounting and Business Research*, *46*(2), 167–195. doi:10.1080/00014788.2015.1039476

Farooq, O., Rupp, D. E., & Farooq, M. (2017). The multiple pathways through which internal and external corporate social responsibility influence organizational identification and multifoci outcomes: The moderating role of cultural and social orientations. *Academy of Management Journal*, *60*(3), 954–985. doi:10.5465/amj.2014.0849

Fatemi, A., Fooladi, I., & Tehranian, H. (2015). Valuation effects of corporate social responsibility. *Journal of Banking & Finance*, *59*, 182–192. doi:10.1016/j.jbankfin.2015.04.028

Flammer, C., & Luo, J. (2017). Corporate social responsibility as an employee governance tool: Evidence from a quasi-experiment. *Strategic Management Journal*, *38*(2), 163–183. doi:10.1002mj.2492

Font, X., Guix, M., & Bonilla-Priego, M. J. (2016). Corporate social responsibility in cruising: Using materiality analysis to create shared value. *Tourism Management*, *53*, 175–186. doi:10.1016/j.tourman.2015.10.007

Frynas, J. G., & Yamahaki, C. (2016). Corporate social responsibility: Review and roadmap of theoretical perspectives. *Business Ethics (Oxford, England)*, *25*(3), 258–285. doi:10.1111/beer.12115

Gupta, A., Briscoe, F., & Hambrick, D. C. (2017). Red, blue, and purple firms: Organizational political ideology and corporate social responsibility. *Strategic Management Journal*, *38*(5), 1018–1040. doi:10.1002mj.2550

Jamali, D., Karam, C., & Blowfield, M. 2017. Introduction: Corporate social responsibility in developing countries: a development-oriented approach. In Development-Oriented Corporate Social Responsibility (vol. 2, pp. 1-12). Routledge.

Lanis, R., & Richardson, G. (2015). Is corporate social responsibility performance associated with tax avoidance? *Journal of Business Ethics*, *127*(2), 439–457. doi:10.100710551-014-2052-8

Lins, K. V., Servaes, H., & Tamayo, A. (2017). Social capital, trust, and firm performance: The value of corporate social responsibility during the financial crisis. *The Journal of Finance*, *72*(4), 1785–1824. doi:10.1111/jofi.12505

Marín, L., Cuestas, P. J., & Román, S. (2016). Determinants of consumer attributions of corporate social responsibility. *Journal of Business Ethics*, *138*(2), 247–260. doi:10.100710551-015-2578-4

Saeidi, S. P., Sofian, S., Saeidi, P., Saeidi, S. P., & Saaeidi, S. A. (2015). How does corporate social responsibility contribute to firm financial performance? The mediating role of competitive advantage, reputation, and customer satisfaction. *Journal of Business Research*, *68*(2), 341–350. doi:10.1016/j.jbusres.2014.06.024

Scherer, A. G., Rasche, A., Palazzo, G., & Spicer, A. (2016). Managing for political corporate social responsibility: New challenges and directions for PCSR 2.0. *Journal of Management Studies*, *53*(3), 273–298. doi:10.1111/joms.12203

Schrempf-Stirling, J., Palazzo, G., & Phillips, R. A. (2016). Historic corporate social responsibility. *Academy of Management Review*, *41*(4), 700–719. doi:10.5465/amr.2014.0137

Su, W., Peng, M. W., Tan, W., & Cheung, Y. L. (2016). The signaling effect of corporate social responsibility in emerging economies. *Journal of Business Ethics*, *134*(3), 479–491. doi:10.100710551-014-2404-4

Taylor, C.R. (2018). *Red alert: On the need for more research on corporate social responsibility appeals in advertising*. Academic Press.

Voegtlin, C., & Greenwood, M. (2016). Corporate social responsibility and human resource management: A systematic review and conceptual analysis. *Human Resource Management Review*, *26*(3), 181–197. doi:10.1016/j.hrmr.2015.12.003

Wang, D. H. M., Chen, P. H., Yu, T. H. K., & Hsiao, C. Y. (2015). The effects of corporate social responsibility on brand equity and firm performance. *Journal of Business Research*, *68*(11), 2232–2236. doi:10.1016/j.jbusres.2015.06.003

Chapter 4
Managing the Risks:
An Observation of Crowd Management and Other Risks Associated With Outdoor Music Festivals in the UK

Wendy C. Sealy
https://orcid.org/0000-0001-6256-9866
University of Chichester, UK

ABSTRACT

Since the 1980s employers in the UK have been subject to statutory responsibilities to ensure that all workplaces are safe. These responsibilities also extend to event managers staging one-off events. The Corporate Manslaughter Act of 1997 and the Health and Safety Act 1999 have invariably changed the way that events are planned, managed, and delivered. This chapter examines best practices for managing major health and safety issues at outdoor music festivals (OMFs) based on an extensive literature review and the author's practitioner experience of various music festivals nationwide. It will provide a practical and convenient reference guide for event managers who do not have time to attend other training or to do extensive research. The first section will discuss the legislative framework for outdoor events in the UK. Next, commentary is provided on the nature and characteristics of outdoor music festivals. Common risks associated with outdoor music festivals are discussed accompanied by actionable steps that event managers can employ to mitigate risks.

DOI: 10.4018/978-1-7998-3230-0.ch004

INTRODUCTION

All employers are subjected to the legal duty to conduct formal risks assessments. The Health and Safety at Work Regulations (1999) makes it a criminal offence for an employer who fails to make suitable arrangements to manage risks. The risk assessment is a critical component of event management for all outdoor festivals. OMFs are associated with increased health and safety risks due, but not limited, to the risk associated with mass crowd gatherings, particularly those including younger demographics. Typical risks include illness due to intoxication, disorder and rioting, crowd surges, stampede and assault. The risk at OMFs is exacerbated due to the influence of music, drugs and alcohol. A range of public health issues such as access to safe drinking water, sanitation facilities, and food borne diseases are also areas of concern (Earl, Parker and Capra, 2005). OMFs usually require extra security and medical services, which can increase the overall costs of hosting the event. Other types of risk posed by outdoor venues may include inadequate provisions for bad weather or lost or stolen valuables (Tangit, KIbat and Adanan, 2016).

While the above researchers agree that there are links between increased public health risks and outdoor music events, these risks can be minimized or eliminated through the proper implementation of risk assessments. The Purple Guide (HSE guide) publication in the UK offers several recommendations for ensuring good health and safety management at outdoor events, but it does not always give explicit guidance on best practices and tactics that could be implemented. Consequently, assessing risks could be intimidating for event mangers who have little experience in risk management. However, understanding and managing crowd behaviour, suppliers and traders is paramount to the safety and success of outdoor festivals (Reid and Ritchie, 2011). Improving the quality of planning, and event management is the best method to deal with risks involving large gatherings (Bladen, Kennel, Abson and Wilde, 2012). Assessing the health and safety risks of major outdoor music festivals forms a crucial plank within the wider framework of event management.

The Legislative Framework for Events in the UK

The Management of Health and Safety at Work (1974) Act imposes a duty on employers to carry out risk assessments to protect workers whose health and safety may be at risk due to work activity. Under the Act, employers are required to have systems and procedures in place to deal with all threats to the health, safety and wellbeing of employees, customers, suppliers and visitors. The Act also requires employers who have five or more employees to have a clear health and safety policy which is displayed in an area where it is visible to all employees (Raj, Walters &

Rashid, 2009). Under the Employers Liability Compulsory Insurance Act (1969) it is also compulsory for all employers to be covered by employer's liability insurance.

Although employer's liability insurance is compulsory it is surprising that taking out public liability insurance is not a legal requirement for companies in the UK. This is alarming as it means that any loss or injury to a person or organisation would come under personal liability, which would put the event manager under significant financial risks, particularly if they are freelancers. Having said that, it is inadvisable not to have public liability insurance cover due to the high degree of complexity and risks involved in staging an outdoor festival. Insurance lessens the financial impacts should a loss be incurred but it does not cover you where there is a breech in safety procedures or if you failed to meet the legal regulations. The majority of venue owners and district councils will insist that the event organiser presents evidence of public liability insurance coverage of a minimum of £5 million alongside an adequate risk assessment before a Temporary Event Notice (TEN) is granted. Some events may need more insurance coverage depending on the nature of the event and the activities involved.

Shone and Parry (2010) recommends that insurance be taken out where possible and these should include public liability insurance, employer's liability insurance and equipment liability insurance. It is also wise to ensure that all suppliers and contractors hired by the event organisers are adequately protected by public liability insurance, employer's liability insurance and equipment liability insurance for all of their activities. The major types of insurable risk are explained below:

Public Liability

Public liability involves claims arising from a third party's property or equipment. It would also involve any incident resulting in injury or illness to a patron or supplier or other persons. Legal liability would also arise in cases when the event manager failed to perform resulting in a breach of duty of care.

Equipment Liability

This would cover damage to equipment which may occur during movement, assembly or dismantling.

Employers Liability

Employers' liability insurance can pay the compensation costs and legal fees if an employee or ex-employee sues for losses arising from illness or injury caused by their work.One of the biggest risks for outdoor events is cancellation due to bad weather. Shone and Parry (2010) suggest that event managers consider insurance to cover the cost of abandonment where severe weather may occur before or during the event leading to cancellation.

The Corporate Manslaughter and Homicide Act (1997) introduced an important element in the corporate management of health and safety. Under the Act an organisation can be found guilty of corporate manslaughter if the way in which it conducts its business causes a death due to a breach of a duty of care to the deceased. The Act penalises organisations who cut costs by taking unjustifiable risks with people's safety. Under the Act prosecutions will be of the corporate body and not individuals, but the liability of directors, board members or other individuals under health and safety law or general criminal law, will be unaffected. The Health and Safety Executive in the UK enforces the Act. Therefore, under the Act organisations that are non-compliant when it comes to health and safety risk significant reputational and financial damage to their organisation.

Additionally, the legal framework for event management in the UK also includes local authorities. If your event is on council property the event manager may have to comply with separate and additional statutory and other regulations before the event can go ahead. Event stakeholders, parent companies and the local district council will need assurances that all risks are minimised for the safe delivery of an event before granting the event organiser the various licenses required for the event to go ahead. Consequently, approval to go ahead with the event could be a long drawn-out and iterative process. It is advisable that event organisers check with the venue owners and district councils regarding any rules and regulations with which they must comply if they are to be granted an event license.

Finally, the event manager will need to ensure that the venue design and layout conforms with all requirements of the Discrimination Disability Act (1995). This may be challenging if an outside venue has uneven terrain requiring temporary ramps and other facilities to be factored into the design. The Act has had far reaching implications for event managers in terms of logistics and cost where outside venues are concerned. Other key legislation and codes of practice governing the events sector in the UK are listed below:

- Corporate Manslaughter Act, 1997
- Health and Safety at Work Act, 1974
- Management of Health and Safety at Work Regulations, 1999
- Workplaces (Health, Safety and Welfare) Regulations, 1992
- Personal Protective Equipment at Work Regulations, 1992
- Provision and Use of Work Equipment Regulations, 1998
- Health and Safety (First Aid) Regulations, 1981

- Reporting of Injuries, Diseases and Dangerous Occurrences Regulations (RIDDOR), 1995
- The Licensing Act, 2003
- Environmental Protection Act, 1990
- Environment Act, 1995
- Manual Handling Operations Regulations, 1992
- Noise at Work Regulations, 1989
- Health and Safety (Signs and Signals) Regulations, 1996
- Building Regulations
- Building Standards Regulations (Scotland)
- NOEAs Code of Practice for Outdoor Events
- Health and Safety Executive (Event Safety Guide), 1999

Source: (Bladen, Kennell, Abson and Wilde, 2012)

The list above, although not exhaustive, demonstrates the sheer myriad of laws, rules and regulations with which the event industry must comply. This could be both intimidating and exhausting. The rules and regulations are also constantly changing which makes it difficult for event organisers to keep up. It is advisable to always consult legal counsel, your district council and other local authorities for advice.

Understanding Crowd Behaviour

Crowd management is usually defined as the set of measures taken in the process of facilitating the movement, comfort and enjoyment of people (Berlonghi, 1995), It involves devising and implementing measures to control the distribution of people over a certain area (Martella, Conrado, Li and Vermeeren, 2017). Crowd management involves profiling and predicting how crowds are going to behave and managing the variables that affect their behaviour. The resulting plan or design for a given event should consider the physical infrastructure, natural environment, the social conditions and operational measures needed for the safety, well-being and enjoyment of the crowd.

The key to competent crowd management involves an understanding of crowd behaviour. Crowd behaviour is different from individual behaviour in that a mass assembly or mass gathering has the potential to move from an orderly crowd into an uncontrollable mob regardless of cultural or economic orientation. Researchers have used various disciplines to understand crowd behaviour including sociological, psychological and environmental factors. From a sociological perspective the behaviour of crowds can be explained in terms of the 'collective consciousness'. When in a crowd the individual loses their individuality and social responsibility. This causes the crowd to become a cohesive and collective force (Silvers, 2008).

Since an event is a collective experience it encourages shared objectives, actions and emotions. When individuals entre into a collective mind-set they exhibit behaviour that is counter to their normal way of acting.

The tourism literature also provides us with an understanding of crowd behaviour from a psychological perspective. Plog (1974) developed two tourists typologies: the allocentric and the psychocentric individual. Allocentric individuals tend to be free with money, take risks, will become bored easily, and wants excitement. The allocentric is the person who would risk climbing on to the stage. The psychocentric individual, in contrasts, wants fun but without danger. They are more reserved, thrifty with money and will tend to complain (Tarlow, 2002). They want to enjoy themselves but without the crowd and dangerous situations. Rock concerts are likely to attract allocentric individuals, particularly where there is a 'mosh pit' and other similar high-energy activities. However, since concerts will attract both types of individuals an event manager should never assume that any crowd is homogenous. An understanding of the crowd characteristics attending an event would help the event manager to better devised plans to manage the crowds. However, event managers should be cognizant that all crowds, regardless of type, have the potential to erupt.

Frustration-aggression theory offers a psychological explanation of crowd behaviour. It suggests that aggressive behaviour can also occur due to frustration, boredom, excessive waiting, discomfort and environmental conditions like heat, cold, noise, ergonomic issues or when expectations are not met. These conditions can trigger the mood of the crowd by creating emotions such as fear, anger or elation which can be exacerbated by alcohol, drugs and the lack of timely and accurate information. Other factors that can cause negative emotions is when there is an interruption in the flow of traffic such as when entering or exiting a venue resulting in a critical crowd pressure point (Raineri, 2005) or frustration caused by no shows, cancellations, lack of parking, lack of information, noise levels or the presence of rival groups (Bladen, Kennel, Abson and Wilde (2012). Incidents can also occur during a flight response to a real or perceived threat that can cause a crush as everyone seeks safety. The risk manager must put in place systems, processes, facilities and services to minimise frustration and should closely monitor and quickly respond to crowd conditions that incite frustration.

From a criminology perspective, continuous minor incidents empower individuals to commit acts that are not acceptable if there is no timely and visible interventions by law enforcement. The failure to address undesirable behaviour immediately encourages others to commit the same infractions. The lack of timely response can lead to the escalation of a situation as happened at the Puerto Rico Day parade in New York City in 2000 when 50 women were sexually molested while the police stood by without acting (Tarlow, 2002).

Canetti (1973) uses analogy to explain crowd behaviour. They contend that a crowd is like fire in that it spreads rapidly, is contagious, is destructive, is insatiable, can break out anywhere and with great suddenness; acts as though it were alive, has multiple parts and is destructive. This view suggests that event managers need to plan for any and every eventuality and must be able to act quickly when it comes to crowd management.

Wijermanns, Conrado, van Steen, Martella and Li (2016) provides a useful conceptual model involving spatial temporal, social and psychological variables for analysing crowd behaviour:

- **Spatio-Temporal Variables**: density, size, position, movement, and acceleration of (parts) of the crowd.
- **Social Variables**: purpose, age distribution, gender distribution, group membership, social structure, leadership, status, and social identity.
- **Psychological-Cognitive Variables**: mood, mindset, intentions, and beliefs.

The model, although by no means exhaustive, can be used as a guide when assessing the risk caused by large crowd gatherings at festivals and other events.

Crowd Management and Outdoor Events

Good crowd management is part of the event experience and starts with the event planning and preparation process (Bala, 2018). The objectives of the event manager should be to provide excellent customer service that ensures the enjoyment, comfort, convenience, safety and security of attendees. Planning should involve a multidisciplinary approach that draws on the perspectives and expertise of a range of individuals. These include the event organizers, crowd managers, police, stewards, first-aid, medical representatives, local district council authorities, transportation operators and crowd simulation experts.

The management of crowds at OMFs are of a much higher level of complexity than planning for an indoor festival (Saragih, Hariandja and Sukoyo, 2016). Outdoor music festivals bring higher risk because they can attract large numbers of young people who may come with little experience of the event and venue. The nature of the acts, popularity of the artists/musicians and the activities available to them may represent significant dangers. Binge drinking, sexual assault and drug use by underage individuals are associated with crowds at OMF (Van Der Wagen and White, 2006). Activities such as the presence of a 'mosh pit' or the serving of alcohol can exacerbate crowd behaviour. Other risks can also come about due to the serving of food which creates the potential for food borne diseases, hygiene and sanitation risks. Additionally, risks are increased due to the use of volunteers and other untrained staff, untried venues, and a range of uncoordinated suppliers (Tum, Norton and Wright, 2006).

Crowd crushing has been identified as a frequent cause of crowd incidents resulting in death at music festivals. The way in which crowds behave and respond is a combination of psychological and environmental factors and will depend on the activities of the crowd and these will be influenced by the character of both the crowd and the groups or artists performing. Tarlow (2002) agree on a list of factors that affect crowd behaviour at festivals. These include:

- The type of event
- The type of venue - if the venue is bounded (fenced and secured) or unbounded
- The duration of the event
- Whether the event is predominantly an outdoor or indoor event
- The crowd mood
- The weather (temperature and humidity)
- Whether the crowd is predominantly seated or mobile or if the event is ticketed or un-ticketed.
- Availability of alcohol and drugs
- Crowd density
- the level of public services and facilities available
- The geography of the event (topography and locality); and
- Average age and gender of the crowd.

Crowd management, is not simply achieved by attempting to control the audience, but by trying to understand their behaviour and the various conditions that affect their behaviour. Each condition listed above is dealt with in the various discussions below.

Venue Design, Layout & Topography

The grounds on which you are to hold the event must be subjected to a risk assessment and safety evaluation A walk-around of the event grounds during the planning process and before the venue is contracted is an astute use of planning time so that areas of concern can be identified, fixed, removed or avoided. Event planners will need to make sure that there is adequate parking bays and disable parking bays for attendees, suppliers, contractors and event staff. Space will be required for the emergency services to entre, exit and rendezvous on the event site. If coaches will be bringing people to the event then parking facilities and rendezvous space will be needed for these vehicles. Key consideration should be given to load-in and load-out and event organisers should ensure that vehicle access to the site facilitates the safe offloading and loading of equipment, particularly heavy or cumbersome equipment.

Scattered arrival and departure times for suppliers and traders can reduce traffic congestion at load-in and load-out. To prevent overcrowding or overlap between pedestrians and vehicles before, during and after the event there should be clear pathways for exclusive pedestrian flow and a one-way traffic system for vehicles. Because outdoor events also lend themselves to intruders any areas that would need to be fenced in would be identified during any preliminary inspection of the venue. Event organisers should also think about possibilities such as traffic accidents and crazy outsiders (probably intoxicated) trying to gain unauthorised entry. Events taking place in high crime or urban areas may be at increased risk of third-party criminal or gang attacks. Event Mangers unfamiliar with the venue environment should do a thorough investigation and take protective measures.

Indoor venues tend to be controlled environments with clear capacity levels and a built-in infrastructure which makes planning easier. However, outdoor venues may represent unfamiliar terrain for the suppliers, contractors and event managers. For example, if there are hidden holes or dips in the ground where visitors, staff or volunteers could fall or twist an ankle, these need to be identified and addressed in advance. Cracks and crevices in the terrain can cause sprains, trips and other injuries. Overhanging branches from trees and shrubbery would need to be dealt with as they could cause face, head and eye injuries. A beautifully landscaped location might be a perfect amphitheatre, but it may not be able to withstand the heavy footfall generated from event visitors. The stomping and jumping of crowds at music festivals can damage grass areas and this damage should be factored into the risk assessment and insurance. Likewise, other sensitive surfaces will have to be protected from damage and the event insurers must be notified. In fact, the terrain should be factored in as a major consideration for insurance purposes.

There are several other public hazards present at outdoor events that would require mitigation. The event manager should be aware of any pools, water courses, swamps, marshes in the area that may present a threat. If there is a pool or body of water nearby there is the potential for accidents and drowning. A body of water can pose problems – especially if there are children in attendance or where liquor is consumed. Warning signs should be in place and the areas should be monitored by security and fenced off to prevent entry.

Outdoor event attendees may also be at risk of insect bites, rodents, snake bites, spiders, wasps, ants, bees, noxious weeds and dust. Silvers (2008: 89) created an extensive list of environmental hazards associated with outdoor events which the event manager must mitigate. The event manager should also consider how the venue terrain and landscape would react to bad weather such as flooding and high winds, hail and rain. Event organisers should choose well drained sites rather than steep, slope and boggy areas (HSE, 1999).

Table 1. Environmental health risks at outdoor events

• Bad weather: high winds, rain, hail, flooding, dust storm, snow, ice • Insect bites, snake bites, spiders • Uneven terrain • Marshes, pools, lakes, cliffs, valleys, swamps • Holes and crevices • Quarries and pits • UV radiation • Excessive cold and heat • Natural gasses & chemicals • Noxious weeds • Grass fires • Poison ivy • Wind-burn • Sun-burn • Hyperthermia • Hypothermia	• Pollution • Dust/dirt • Rodents • Excessive noise • Domesticated animals • Wild animals • Chemicals • Contamination • Infectious diseases • Neighbouring land use • Drugs & alcohol use • Failing temporary infrastructure • Wells & suck holes/blow holes • Contaminated drinking water • Sanitation • Wells • Exhaustion • dehydration

Environmental Risks

Outdoor events can be literally "taken out" through bad weather. Bad weather can turn a 'feast crowd' into a 'fleeing crowd' (Tarlow, 2002) as visitors scamper for shelter from rain, hail, high winds, thunder and lightning. Flooding and earthquakes should also be taken into consideration. Bad weather can also destroy your rental equipment and blow away and destroy furniture, marquess, gazebos and inflatables. Even on a sunny dry day, high winds should not be taken lightly and in severe cases the event should be cancelled or abandoned and the site evacuated. Windblown equipment can cause damage to other equipment and injury to attendees, staff and volunteers. The consequences of damage and injury caused by bad weather could have legal and financial implications. Taking the advice of the metrological office and the local authorities is paramount to everyone's safety. Your risk assessment should include a clear plan for site abandonment and an orderly crowd emergency evacuation in case the weather takes a turn for the worse.

Event communications to staff and visitors should recommend that individuals dress for hot and cold and wet and dry weather at the same time. Free drinking water should be available to prevent dehydration and guests and staff should be advised to guard against sunburn. In the UK it can snow in April or a heat wave could occur in the middle of winter. It is recommended that portable heaters be available for events near the change of seasons. Below (table 1) is a range of environmental risks that would need to be planned for.

Venue Infrastructure and Accessibility

The venue should be assessed for the provision of running water, toilets, electricity and lighting. Buildings that could be used for offices, communication outposts or medical services should be identified and evaluated for suitability, safety, practicality and logistics. It the venue is in a remote location a water and electrical supply may need to be installed. Event planners would then need to consider the number and size of water tanks that would be needed and the number and type of generators that would be required. Consideration of the layout and the areas that would need lighting and electrical generators should be reviewed during the planning stage.

The geographical location of the venue will be a crucial factor in the management of health and safety. Consideration should be given to the proximity of the nearest hospital, fire and police services should there be an emergency. Good accessibility to reliable and frequent public transport, major roads and highways, parking and local services will make logistical planning much easier than in a remote location. The event manager would also want to establish if there are any hazards such as rivers or lakes or any gas pipes running through the area. By walking the site and by studying the topography and site plans the event manager would be able to beforehand identify any potential risks that would need mitigation. Many of these hazards will be identified when evaluating the site and will require the event manager to implement healthy safeguards to mitigate against the above risks.

In addition to the above, many other factors in the design and planning of the event will have a bearing on crowd management. These may include the layout and design of the venue to allow smooth and fast entry and exits, and space for crowd movement including queuing and emergency evacuation. The risk analysis should make provision for the phases of arrival, departure, queuing, capacity levels and evacuation as separate activities (Upton, 2008). The adequate supply and spread out of facilities such as toilets, catering and refreshments and sanitary facilities should all be considered.

It is important to recognised that venue capacity, crowd size and density is a major factor in crowd management and it is at this point in planning that event managers should determine the size of the audience that the site can accommodate. This decision should take into consideration the space that is required for a temporary infrastructure such as stage, toilets, mobile catering, tents and marquess and control points and should be made in consultation with space experts and the local fire and council authorities. Most of the crowd disasters in history have occurred due to overcrowding causing crowd compression and the subsequent loss of footing, or inability to move resulting in injuries and fatalities (Silvers, 2008). At the site planning stage, it is important that adequate space for congregation and circulation is factored into the site plans. Upton (2008) recommends a formula of 2 persons per square meter. People need space to move around and to see where they are going. The thoughtful positioning of infrastructure, services and activities during planning can reduce congestion.

Toilets

The Workplace (Health, Safety and Welfare) Regulations (1992) specify the requirements for the provision of sanitation and welfare facilities (including toilets) for people at work. It is appropriate to provide an adequate number and the right type of toilets for the number of people expected to attend the event, including provisions for disable persons and all staff, volunteers, contractors and suppliers. For events involving children the event manager should provide baby changing facilities.

The numbers and locations of toilets should be agreed with the licensing authorities. The table below is a general guideline for music events based on the recommendations of the HSE (1999):

1 toilet should be provided per 100 females and 1 toilet per 120 females if the event lasts more than 6 hours. 1 toilet should be provided per 500 males, plus 1 urinal per 150 males. If the event lasts more than 6 hours organisers should provide 1 toilet per 600 males, plus 1 urinal per 175 males.Event managers should consider demographics, gender and if there will be a high fluid consumption like alcohol which will require a greater number of toilets to be provided. Events involving camping would require even more facilities including showers. For large festivals the built-in toilets of the venue may be insufficient so the event manager may have to hire in portable toilets. If this is the case then provision for safe and hygienic waste removal must be arranged. Consideration should be given to the location, access, construction, type of temporary facilities, lighting and signage. The locations of toilet facilities should be spread out across the site rather than located in one main location. An even distribution of facilities across the site will allow for better queue control and less congestion and traffic in any one area.

The HSE (1999) states that you must provide handwashing facilities of no less than 1 per 10 toilets with warm water, soap and hand drying facilities. Event managers should make provisions to ensure that toilets are monitored regularly for safety, hygiene, cleaning and the replenishment of toilet paper, soap and hand towels. Antiseptic hand wipes or bacterial soap should be provided where warm water is not available but should not be used as a substitute for water. An adequate number of toilet facilities for disabled persons would need to be provided as well as rubbish bins around the site where they will be required.

Alcohol Management at Outdoor Events

Events where alcohol is sold may face various problems such as unruly crowd behaviour, riots and sexual and other types of assault. Alcohol sales puts the event manager in a perilous position. Alcohol and drug use can contribute to aggressive behaviour and make managing crowds more difficult for the event manager. Event managers must consider the audience profile and crowd dynamics in their crowd management plans. A 'feast crowd' can easily turn into a mob as drinking releases undesirable urges that can instigate a multitude of destructive behaviours. Ritchie and Reid (2017) list several risks associated with the sale of alcohol:

- Personal injury and loss due to criminal acts and drunkenness
- Lewd behaviour
- Additional insurance cost against possible lawsuits against the event, its suppliers and agents.
- Additional security cost
- Additional clean-up and restoration cost
- Vandalism
- Destination image problems and consequential loss of reputation and future patronage

Tarlow (2002) adds to the list and warns that events which host young people are likely to risk the occurrence of:

- Driving while intoxicated
- Date rape and rape drugs dropped into drinks and other types of sexual assault
- Mixing of alcohol and drugs
- The tendency to brawl or fight and illegal hazing.
- Sexual harassment, obscene gestures or touching, pinching or patting
- Violence
- Threats to staff and volunteers
- Paranoia
- Romantic obsessions or statements

While event managers may be tempted to allow alcohol sales at their events due to the financial gain, UK law holds the event manager liable for any injury or death a third party may suffer as a result of intoxicated persons. Event organisers must carefully consider the distribution, sale and consumption of alcohol and put security measures in place to prevent excessive alcohol and drug consumption. A strict alcohol policy must be enforced and a separate alcohol risk assessment should be done with key consideration given to crowd behaviour, the loss of property, the type of acts (some acts incite violence and lewd behaviour) and the level of security and type of medial provision that will be required. Alcohol sales will guarantee that some patrons will become ill and will need medical attention. Illness reported by festival goers due to alcohol consumption include vomiting, heatstroke and collapsing (Feltmann, Elgan and Gripenberg, 2019). An ambulance service as well as paramedics and a sick bay would be needed for those who need treatment. Security will also need to be vigilant in case of violent outbreaks and assault. The serving of alcohol will invariably ensure that there will be crowd incidents. It is probably better to omit the serving of alcohol, if viable, as the extra security, medical services and insurance required increases the overall cost of the event (Tangit, Kibat and Adanan, 2016; Wertheimer, 1993).

Outdoor events lend themselves to intruders and gate-crashers. Even if you have entry/exit procedures you should also think about other possibilities such as crazy outsiders who are inebriated entering the event and causing a disturbance. Even family events can lend themselves to inebriated individuals who could gate crash the event and make it unpleasant for other visitors. At events where alcohol is prohibited, organisers may need security to take extra precautions such as searching personal belongings at the gates to confiscate any alcohol, drugs and weapons being smuggled through the gates of the event.

It is important that volunteers and performers are not allowed to drink alcohol or consumed drugs in the 24 hours before and during their shift or performance. This requirement should be written into their employment contracts. Alcohol should not be sold where there are foreseeable crowd problems and age restrictions should be strictly observed (Abbot and Geddie, 2001). A strong security presence will be needed in the areas where alcohol is sold. Under UK law a 'personal licenced holder' must be available to oversee and manage the sale of alcohol. The risks associated with alcohol consumption are too numerous to mention in this paper, however table 4.2, below, summarises several additional risks.

Where alcohol is sold the event manger should seek advice from the medical team and put measures in place to minimise its effects. Lyne and Galloway (2011) recommends that having food high in protein available and avoiding salty foods will help to reduce the effects of alcohol. By having specific ending and start times for the selling of alcohol and having non-alcoholic drinks available can limit the sale and consumption of alcohol and its effects.

Tarlow (2002) advises that event managers should focus on designing events on which the focus is on an amazing theme and customer experience rather than the drinking of alcohol. Programming should encourage event visitors to engage with other activities - games, speeches, competitions etc. which will divert their attention from drinking. Event managers should not depend on alcohol sales as the major

Table 2. Other risks associated with alcohol sales at events/festivals

Risks to Visitors/ spectators	Risks to event staff	Risk to the event organisers
• Moves to coerce sexual relations • Staring at another person's private parts • Unwanted whistling • Uninvited comments about a gender trait • Sexually suggestive sounds • Statements about a person's sexual parts or sex life • Continual requests for sexual favours • Cursing & swearing • Gate crashers • Gunfire • Knife attacks • Theft • Crowd crushing • Drug abuse • Arrest • Fighting	• Threats to staff or attempts to intimidate staff • Overtly moral righteousness statements • Blaming others for one's mistakes • Gunfire • Knife attacks • Altercations between staff & attendees • Assault	• Risk of 3rd party lawsuits • Gunfire • Bad reputation • Event cancellation/abandonment • Financial loss • Bad press • Banned from venue/location/country/ destination • Vandalism • Inadequate security • Corporate liability

source of income as this lends itself to decisions based on conflicts of interest - mainly financial gain. Focussing on multiple income streams for the event through charging for fringe activities, merchandising, food sales, space rentals, sponsorship, and other commercial activities should reduce the focus on alcohol sales for income. If alcohol is sold a major public education campaign directed towards festival goers should be in place. For example, pamphlets could be used to warn festival goers of the dangers of alcohol and drug use, how to drink and drive safely and what to do if a friend is inebriated.

Considering the reputational and financial risk that alcohol sales create, the event manager should perhaps consider the wider ethical issues and ask themselves whether the problems associated with alcohol consumption and the reputational damage that it could bring resonates with the values, ethos and image of the event and product they wish to create. One negative incident can negatively influence future visits to the planned event and the location for several years after the incident has taken place (Ritchie and Reid, 2017). Table 3 summarises measures that can be taken to reduce the consumption of alcohol and its effects.

Table 3. Tactics to limit the effects of alcohol consumption

• Have set start and finish times for the serving of alcohol • Have non-alcoholic drinks and water available • Have alcohol policy in place • Limit alcohol sales per person • Follow all local laws and procedures • Have foods that are high in protein (The higher the protein, the higher the food functions to reduce the effects of alcohol) • Have drinking water available • Have pamphlets to warn patrons of dangers associated with alcohol consumption • Enforcement of ID credentials • Ban alcohol from the 'mosh pits' • Avoid advertising alcohol as an event attraction • Set up alcohol free zones within the event arena • Have a strong police and security presence	• Refrain from serving salty foods • Only use cash bars • Use of portion controls and serving size limits • Keep the audience occupied. (If people are bored they may be inclined to drink more) • Appoint stewards to monitor for intoxicated people • Have coffee available • Have a medical team and sick bay available • Develop a 'drink safe-drive safe' policy • Guard against alcohol being smuggled into the venue • Avoid sponsors who are alcohol manufacturers • Publicise a no-nonsense event policy • Use a drink ticketing system • Refuse entry to intoxicated people • Search visitors at gates to confiscate any smuggling of alcohol into the event

Source: (Lyne and Galloway, 2011; Neighbors, Walters, Lee, Vader, Vehige, Szigethy, DeJong, 2007; Silvers, 2008; Tarlow 2002; Van der Wagen and White, 2006).

Crowd Management & Security Deployment

People's mood and emotions such as excitement, desperation, frustration, hysteria and aggression may affect their behaviour. Audiences who are not satisfied with the performance of a pop group may react with abuse or aggression or may become uncooperative or offensive. Likewise, if people are delayed trying to enter a venue they may become impatient and start jumping over barriers. It is thus essential that event managers put measures in place to combat against such occurrences.

Unfortunately, some artists' activities such as diving or throwing items into the audience and performing in the audience arena can have negative impacts. The event manager would need to decide if they want to allow certain activities as part of any performance and include them in the risk assessment. All performances, including lyrics should be censored to ensure that all performances resonate with the ethos and values of the event and are suitable for the intended audience, especially if children will be in attendance.

The known actions of performers should be researched to determine if they have a reputation for instigating high density crowd activity. These activities include 'moshing', 'diving', 'shanking', 'pogoing', 'surfing', and 'swirling'. Such activities are notorious for causing lateral or dynamic surges, crowd swirls, crowd collapses or localised high density, all of which might subject the crowd into dangerously high pressure loads (Raineri, 2005). Event managers should consider banning these activities from the event altogether and ensure that their prohibition is explicitly stated in performers contracts. Upton (2008) warns that in cases of crowd disturbances and accidents caused by performers that the performers' lawyers will try to make a case for the blame to be placed on the local security team, the venue manager or event manager or all other parties. In such cases the venue manager, event manager and security team would need to present unambiguous evidence of duty of care through risk assessments, the implementation of risk management strategies and staff training records. It is important to conduct a comprehensive risk assessment for each of these activities if they are likely to take place. Adequate security, assisted by stewards and close monitoring by CCTV, video and photographic evidence will be essential to ensure that these activities do not cause harm or bring about reputational, financial and psychological lost for the organisers.

Crowd mood is also influenced by changes in the tempo or rhythm of songs Earl, Parker and Capra, 2005: Tangit, Kibat and Adanan, 2016; Wertheimer, 1993). Heavy metal rock, hardcore punk, rap and high percussion Caribbean calypso, 'dub' and 'soca' are considered highly influential on crowd behaviour. It is important that stewards are able to recognise changes in crowd mood so that they can act before a disturbance ensues.

Hiring and Deploying Security

The Private Security Industry Act (2001) was implemented in 2006. The purpose of this act was to remove rogue security companies that permeate the entertainment and leisure industries. Before hiring any venue or security company, it is vital that the event manager ascertain the legal status of the security staff who will be employed by the company or venue. It is an offence to employ security staff who have not been trained, security checked by the police and who do not have the license for the designated task to be carried out (Raj, Walters and Rashid, 2017). The local police can provide a list of all vetoed security in your area, but the event manager can also ask the security company to provide all certificates and licenses and evidence of training for the personnel who will be working at the event. These documents should be kept in the event statutory folder and then matched against the security persons who show up to work at the event. If an event is expected to attract children, then all security personnel should be DBS checked and copies of these reports should be kept in the statutory event folder.

The number and type of security required will depend on the numbers of attendees, the activities on offer and the nature of the event. A professional security firm can assist in making these decisions based on their experience, but the final decision is that of the event organisers and local authorities. A good security presence in clearly identifiable uniforms such as high vis jackets is vital to making people feel safe and to deter people from undesirable behaviour. The use of undercover security can also be advantageous when it comes to uncovering criminal activity or drug crimes. It is also important that there is a contingency team of security persons and stewards available to deal with unforeseen events and emergencies. This avoids removing security and stewards from areas that require a security presence to deal with emergencies in other areas of the venue.

Security guards will need to be deployed to areas where alcohol is being consumed and sold. Security should also look out for the use of illegal drugs so that the risk of injury and other crowd problems can be reduced. Security personnel should be trained to recognise the various types of drugs and the symptoms associated with their use. An undercover presence is best for detecting the use of illegal drugs and security guards should be strategically placed in dark corners and car parks and other suspicious areas where drugs are likely to be consumed (Abbot and Geddie, 2001).

When deciding on the level of security presence needed the event manager should take into consideration, the demographic profile of the crowds, crowd history at the event and the history of crowd reaction to the planned performers. Crowd activities such as a 'mosh pit' and 'diving' will need extra security. A heavy security presence may be required at the entrances and exits and security should be deployed in the middle of the crowds in various areas of the arena. Event managers should also consider that during peak times bars and food outlets may be busy and will become areas of potential hazards for the movement of the crowd. These areas may require extra security and stewards during peak times. It is important that organisers recognise that it may become necessary to usher crowds into alternative, previously identified contingency spaces in order to ensure an equal distribution of people and to avoid overcrowding other areas. It is important that stewards are trained to execute these duties competently and confidently. It is important to recognised that OMFs are attended by large numbers of individuals who attend in groups hence, they will tend to move around together, stop and chat in pedestrian pathways and to arrive and leave together. Attention needs to be paid to these individuals as they could cause an obstacle for the movement of others around the site and become a problem of crowd control (Raj, Walters and Rashid, 2017). For very high-risk events a police presence may be necessary but note that the police may charge for this service.

Surveillance cameras (CCTV) can be monitored by security staff in a control room. These can provide valuable extra security for events over a large area (Martella, Conrado, Li and Vermeeren, 2017). CCTV can aid the monitoring and counting of people in small areas around the event site, the space between people, the rate of flow into or out of an area, the overall number and distribution of people in the crowd, the general crowd mood, signs of distress, pushing or surging, indications of bad temper or excitement as well as any signs of other potential crowd problems. CCTV can also detect areas where extra security may be required. Other monitoring systems and strategies would include the deployment of helicopters and unmanned aerial vehicles equipped with video cameras and turnstiles linked to automatic counting systems (*Ibid).*

Managing Traffic Flow and Avoiding Congestion

Crowd and pedestrian dynamics not only play a major role when the crowd arrive at and leave the site, but also throughout the duration of the event. When designing the layout of event venues, multiple routes, entrances and exits should be factored into the ground plans. Attractions should be spread out evenly over the entire site rather than concentrated in one area to allow an even distribution of traffic across the site and to prevent any one area from becoming congested. At some events a temporary infrastructure may be put in place to manage pedestrian traffic. For instance, barriers, fences, turnstiles, pathways and signage can help to guide people along certain routes. Stewards will be the essential force in ensuring that there are no bottlenecks or long queues. Earl, Parker and Capra (2005) recommends that event managers should check sites for steep slopes, dead ends, the convergence of routes, uneven or slippery flooring and the placement of facilities throughout the site (e.g. food outlets, bars, and toilets). It is also necessary to watch for reverse flows, obstructions created by queues or gathering crowds, pedestrian flows mixing with vehicular traffic, and moving attractions within the crowd (Raineri 2005). Finally, ensuring there is continuous electricity for lighting within the site, on internal and external pathways leading to and from the site and in car parks will assist in keeping patrons feeling safe and secure.

Ingress/Egress

Event Managers should ensure that entrances and exits are clearly signposted and operate efficiently. There should be a continuous flow of traffic within ingress and egress points. The needs of children and people with mobility difficulties should be considered. It is best to establish multiple ingress and egress points in order to avoid congestion. There should also be separate entrances and exits for pedestrians from the entry routes used by emergency services, and concession vehicles. Upton (2008:4) recommends five (5) key considerations for planning ingress and egress flow and queuing:

- Pedestrian approach to a queue
- Standing space within the queue
- Unrestricted forward movement
- Passing through an egress system
- Dispersal

At OMFs problems may occur at entry points if large numbers of people seek to gain admission at the same time and if not properly managed this may result in crushing injuries, delays or congestion. It is therefore recommended that multiples ingress and egress points are opened several hours before the event is due to start and the audience is made aware of this by social media, tele or radio communications, tickets, posters, billboards or other means (HSE, 1999). It is important to appreciate that when entrances are opened early the audience demands on facilities and services will commence so it is important to have waste clearing, toilets, information and first aid points and catering ready ahead of time. Crowd pressure at the entrances can be reduced by keeping all activities, attractions and catering services well clear of entry points. Queuing areas should be kept away from entrances. Crowds in long queues can be managed by keeping people entertained through strolling entertainers, music and screens to distract them from long waiting times (Bladen, Kennell, Abson and Wilde, 2012). Signage should be used to indicate the length of the queues and marshals can be used to provide information and apologies about the length of waiting, if necessary. Recent technologies have introduced virtual queuing where a customer can enter a queue via their mobile phone. Once they come close to the front of the line they will be notified by way of an alert at which time they can make their way to the event (*Ibid*). This type of technology can be very effective in crowd management.

Event managers need to be mindful that once the doors are opened to the audience people tend to rush towards the front of the stage which can cause tripping accidents and injuries. They should consider how the area in front of the stage will be managed when the entrances are opened. One recommended method of easing the initial rush towards the stage and preventing slipping or tripping accidents is to provide a line or lines of stewards across the arena through which the audience can move towards the stage.

The event managers should ensure that all emergency exits are unlocked, free of obstructions and properly sign posted. Stewards should be assigned to keep all escape routes clear and to ensure that all emergency lighting, fire-fighting equipment and alarms are working. Clear lines of communication need to be established with the audience. This could be a PA system for use in emergencies that can be heard clearly in all parts of the venue. It is also important to have contingency communications equipment available in case of a power cut or the breakdown of generators. In such cases a portable mega phone should be available. The MC can be used to convey information to the audience about delays, cancellations, attractions, emergency routes etc. The table 4, below, includes several strategies for managing crowds at outdoor music festivals

Event Communications

Visual and audible communications are important for effective crowd management. Communication should be visible, clear, specific, concise, courteous, correct, unambiguous, complete and timely in order to prevent dangerous situations from arising.

Electronic communication through the use of two-way radios, cell phones, instant messaging, and the internet bring significant benefits to event managers and aid communications on large sites where written and verbal communication may be difficult. Event managers should never rely solely on technology for communications and should always have a contingency in place in case technology fails. Generators should always be available in case of a power cut and chargers should be available to re-charge dead radios. It is advisable to have on site a number of portable hand-held megaphones in case all else fails.

The event programme book and pamphlets could be used as an effective method of communicating event safety advise and evacuation instructions. Information regarding evacuation procedures, the location of evacuation exits and assembly points, things and places to avoid, location of first aid and information points, emergency telephone numbers and general safety information can be communicated through these sources. Event tickets can be used as a source of communications. Many events now include a small site-plan on the back of tickets. Tickets can be coloured coded to indicate entrance via the corresponding colour coded entrance.

A highly visible information desk can provide information on the location of the various services available to event visitors. The information desk can also serve as a lost child point and a lost property point. It should be staffed by well-informed event staff who are very familiar with the event services and the site-plan, health and safety and who are empowered to make decisions. At very large events more than one information desk may be necessary.

Table 4. Tactics used in crowd management

Capacity Management
• Conform with local laws and codes of practice • Use 2 persons per sq. metre • Provide adequate space for walking, standing and congregating • Identify contingency spaces in case of overcrowding • Sell advanced paid for or free tickets • Use turnstiles & clickers to estimate crowd capacity in spaces • Use fences, barricades to control flow of traffic in specific areas • Keep people moving • Keep people entertained – avoid boredom
Queuing
• Ensure queues do not converge with pedestrian pathways • Provide entertainment to distract from waiting times • Use virtual queuing systems • Use barriers to separate from other service areas • Use signage and other communications to keep people informed • Separate general admission queues from premium admission and VIP admission
Pedestrian Flow
• Introduce a one-way pedestrian traffic flow system • Monitor crowds from above rather than below • Distribute activities across the entire site • Distribute services such as toilets and catering throughout the site • Screen and bar off all out of bound/no go areas • Use signage to direct people • Use well trained and customer focussed stewards to direct people • Ensure aisles and pathways for disable access • Install CCTV • Separate rival groups • Use adequate lighting to avoid hazards and maximise security • Avoid potential stressors – excessive waiting, overcrowding, overwhelming security • Keep people moving • Keep people moving using laughter rather than force • Monitor crowds from above rather than below
Vehicle Movement
• Impose speed limits on vehicles (5 mls per hour) • Marshalls should escort vehicles around the site. One marshal in front and one at the back. • Separate pedestrian and vehicle traffic pathways should be provided • Close event site to vehicular traffic if viable • Allow service vehicles only on site • Assist pedestrians in crossing streets/ pathways
Mosh-Pit Activities
• Separate mosh pit from other event sections • Staff adequately with security, stewards and medical personnel • Ban certain activities such as body slamming, body surfing etc • Monitor for drugs/alcohol usage • Monitor for sexual assault • Hand out pamphlets about most pit dangers • Use signage to warn people of possible mosh pit injuries

Signage

Signage is one of the most effective forms of communication and crowd management. An event site will require different types of signage. Statutory signage includes signage that is required by law such as emergency exits, 'wet floor' and toilets. Directional signage serves to direct visitors around a sight and is good for managing traffic flow. Signage can be used to warn, instruct and inform attendees. Signage can communicate potential hazards to visitors, such as wet or slippery surfaces or can direct a crowd around a venue. Signage should be clear, concise, unambiguous, well written and must be readily recognisable for maximum effects. Signage should be strategically placed around the event site at sight level so that the signage would be recognisable and seen by visitors. Signage placed too high or too low would go unnoticed by attendees.

Medical Cover

The HSE (1999) claims that 1-2% of an audience will seek medical assistance during an event day. They further claim that of these, around 10% will need further treatment on site. Approximately 1% of the number requiring initial medical assistance will require referral to hospital. The number of people requiring medical treatment at any music event will depend on the environmental conditions. Treatment can range from injuries due to crushing, falls, fighting or conditions such as hyperventilation, exhaustion, dehydration, sunstroke, hyperthermia or hypothermia, emotional or anxiety attacks, food poisoning or the serious effects of drugs or alcohol. People with disabilities and existing medical conditions such as asthma, diabetes, heart, or psychiatric problems may attend events where their condition could be worsened. Medical emergencies such as heart attack or stroke will need to be provided for. It is therefore advisable to have an ambulance service on site. It is essential that all major music events have suitable arrangements for the treatment, and transport of those in need.

The recommended minimum number of first-aiders at small events with no special risks is 2:1000 for the first 3000 attending. No event should have less than two first aiders (HSE, 1999). However, some events will need more coverage. The number of first-aiders required will be determined by the nature of the event and the activities planned. There should also be medical coverage during the load-in and load-out to cover suppliers, staff, contractors and volunteers in case of illness or injury during set-up and strike.

The event organiser should also consider the provision of an air ambulance if the event venue is in a remote area or if the nearest hospital is miles away. The risk assessment may indicate the need for the provision of medical practitioners to be on site which may include paramedics, nurses and doctors, particularly if alcohol is served. It is also customary to have on hand a separate medical team who may be in charge of looking after performers, VIPs and/or event staff and volunteers. At events over 6 hours or for very large events, consideration should be given to the provision of a psychiatric team to include psychiatrists, psychiatric nurses and drug counsellors (HSE, 1999). The area immediately in front of the stage should have a rescue board and cervical collars, oxygen therapy, resuscitation equipment and fire extinguishers in case of an incident.

Managing Suppliers & Contractors.

It is difficult to control the activities, policies and methods of working of suppliers and contractors and thus it is important to insist that all contractors and suppliers provide information on systems, procedures and documents that evidence their duty of care and statutory responsibilities. As an event manager you have the authority to insist that all suppliers and contractors have adequate risk assessments for their business that covers the protection of equipment and the health and safety of the public. In the UK most district councils will insist that all contractors and suppliers obtain a minimum of £5million pounds public liability insurance and employers' liability insurance. All supplier and contractor risk assessments should be checked with a fine toothcomb by the event manager to ensure that they adequately cover all risks. Event managers should ensure that all artists, venues, entertainers, entertainer agencies, contractors, security firms, staffing agencies, caterers, builders, contractors, suppliers of equipment etc. are fully insured.

Managing Caterers & Hygiene Standards

Although many may consider food provision to be unrelated to crowd management, the fact is that a mass outbreak of a food borne disease can have the same impact as a mass crushing event in that it can result in death.

Food is a major part of the event experience; however, mobile catering can be risky if caterers do not have the correct equipment and if staff are not trained in hygiene practices. An outbreak of food positioning can have a devastating effect on the event's reputation, ruin the enjoyment of those affected and put pressure on the medical team. In addition, a mass outbreak of food positioning can lead to multiple law suits.

It is not always possible for event mangers to police how all food is sourced, transported, prepared and served. However, some simple steps can help to mitigate the risk of food poisoning and any litigation that the event manager may face as a result of a food disease outbreak. It is recommended that you ensure that all caterers provide documented evidence of:

- Staff hygiene training at a minimum of level 2.
- Public liability insurance of a minimum of £5 million
- Employer's liability insurance of a minimum of £5 million
- Equipment liability insurance of a minimum of $5 million
- Adequate risk assessments to cover the proper transport, preparation and serving of food.

All the above documents should be kept in the event statutory folder. It is important that you hire reputable caterers. Ask for references where appropriate and it is also recommended that you only contract catering operators with a food hygiene rating of no less than 4 stars. Some district councils in the UK will insist on a minimum of a 5-stars rating for events on their land and some will insist that the food rating inspection from which the rating was assigned be conducted within the last 12 months. Always check with your district council or local authorities for advice.

On the day of the event it is important that health and safety checks are carried out by someone appointed by the event manager. These health and safety checks should ensure that all suppliers are operating according to their risk assessments and employing overall safe practices as recommended by The Hazzard Analysis Critical Control Points (HACCP). It is also recommended that catering safety checks are done on a one/two-hour cycle during the event and all observations should be kept in a log. HACCP provides guidelines on the potential hazards associated with food and critical points where hazards can be eliminated. It establishes procedures to monitor control points and to verify systems. Event managers should ensure that all caterers follow the procedures recommended in HACCP. This could be checked by carefully reviewing the risk assessments of all caterers contracted for food services in advance of the event. When checking risk assessments event organisers should ensure that procedures such as the wearing of gloves, the wearing of hats and hairnets and brightly coloured band-aids are part of the procedures (Tum, Norton & Wright, 2006). The proper cooking and storage of food at the right temperatures should be in accordance with HACCP.

In the UK The Food Standards Agency is responsible for assessing the hygiene levels of restaurants, takeaways, food shops, and cafes. It is recommended that event managers check the hygiene rating of caterers on the Food Standards Agency website before any contracts are signed. Additionally, it is important to ensure that the hygiene certificates on file for staff correspond with the staff who actually show up to work in catering on the day of the event. Furthermore, catering staff who exhibit any signs of the flu or colds should be removed from food handling responsibilities.

The event manager, in discussion with the caterers, can also eliminate food risk further by identifying foods with inherent contaminants such as poultry, seafood and dairy. These foods should be given special attention in risk assessments because although they may be safe when cooked properly, hazardous substances may be left on the preparation areas that must be cleaned and sanitised properly to prevent cross contamination. In certain instances, it may be best to eliminate these foods altogether from the event menu. Catering risk assessments should also guard against hazards such as burns, cuts, slips, trips, falls and the safe use of liquid petroleum gas (LPG). Table 5 shows possible sources of food contamination that the event manager would need to address.

Table 5. Sources of Food Contamination

• Poor personal hygiene • Bacteria • Food handlers • Ingredience • Broken/worn equipment • Domesticated animals (dogs, cats) • Food containers • Improper cooling and heating • Food contact surfaces • Foreign objects (hair, stones, dirt, metal, staples, wood, bandages, broken glass, broken finger nails) • Viruses • Improper sanitation • Improper preparation • Improper transportation	• Pesticides • Chemicals • Rodents & insects • Packaging • Equipment breakdown/malfunction • Polluted water • Toxins • Spoilage • Improper stock rotation • Incorrect labelling • Improper sanitation • Improper storage • Cigarette, tobacco smoke • Deliberate contamination by staff (sabotage)

Adapted from: Silvers (2008); Van der Wagen and White (2006,)

CONCLUSION

This chapter covers the wide spectrum of issues associated with managing crowds effectively at OMFs. These issues are however not exhaustive as the scope and word restrictions of this chapter precludes us from covering all contingencies in crowd management. It is advisable that the event manager make themselves aware of all possible scenarios, laws, regulations and issues associated with their event genre and make plans to mitigate them. Consulting crowd management experts, security firms, local authorities, legal experts and event stakeholders will allow the coordination necessary for a safe event to take place.

REFERENCES

Abbott, J., & Geddie, M. W. (2001). Event and venue management: Minimizing liability through effective crowd management techniques. *Event Management*, *6*(4), 259–270. doi:10.3727/152599500108751417

Bala, K. (2018, July-September). Crowd management issues and challenges. *International Journal of Research and Analytical Reviews*, *5*(3), 947–951.

Berlonghi, A. (1995). Understanding and planning for different spectator crowds. *Safety Science*, *18*(4), 239–247. doi:10.1016/0925-7535(94)00033-Y

Bladen, C., Kennell, J., Abson, E., & Wilde, N. (2012). *Events Management: An Introduction*. Oxon: Routledge. doi:10.4324/9780203852972

Canetti, E. (1973). *Crowds and Power*. New York: Farrar Straus Giroux.

Earl, C., Parker, E., & Capra, M. (2005). The management of crowds and other risks at outdoor music festivals: A review of the literature. *Environmental Health*, *5*(1), 37–49.

Feltmann, K., Elgan, T.H. & Gripenberg, J. (2019). High levels of alcohol intoxication and strong support for restrictive alcohol policies among music festival goers. *Substance Abuse Treatment, Prevention, and Policy, 14*(15).

HSE. (1999). Health and safety executive. In *The event safety guide: a guide to health, safety and welfare at music and similar events*. Norwich: HSE.

Lyne, M., & Galloway, A. (2011). Strategies for managing alcohol at large events in New Zealand. *Education, Prevention & Policy, 18*(6).

Martella, C., Conrado, C., Li, J., & Vermeeren, C. (2017). On current crowd management practices and the need for increased situation awareness, prediction, and intervention. *Safety Science*, *91*, 381–393. doi:10.1016/j.ssci.2016.09.006

Neighbors, C., Walters, S. T., Lee, C. M., Vader, A. M., Vehige, T., Szigethy, T., & DeJong, W. (2007). Event-specific prevention: Addressing college student drinking during known windows of risk. *Addictive Behaviors*, *32*(11), 2667–2680. doi:10.1016/j.addbeh.2007.05.010 PMID:17616260

Plog, S. C. (1974). Why destination areas rise and fall in popularity. *The Cornell Hotel and Restaurant Administration Quarterly*, *14*(4), 55–58. doi:10.1177/001088047401400409

Raineri, A. (2005). *The causes and prevention of serious crowd injuries and fatalities at outdoor music festivals.* Retrieved on 20 August 2019 from https://www.researchgate.net/publication/236838507_The_Causes_and_Prevention_of_Serious_Crowd_Injury_and_Fatalities_at_Outdoor_Music_Festivals

Raj, R., Walters, P., & Rashid, T. (2009). *Events Management: An Integrated and Practical Approach*. London: Sage.

Raj, R., Walters, P., & Rashid, T. (2017). *Events Management: Principles & Practice*. London: Sage.

Reid, S., & Ritchie, B. (2011). Risk management: Event managers' attitudes, beliefs, and perceived constraints. *Event Management, 15*(4), 329–341. doi:10.3727/152599511X13175676722528

Ritchie, B., & Reid, S. (2017). Risk Management. In N. Ferdinand & P. Kitchin (Eds.), Events Management: An International Approach (pp. 211-240). Los Angeles: Sage.

Saragih, H. S., Hariandja, E. S., & Sukoyo, S. (2016). Risk Management Design for Private, Small, and Medium Scale Musical Concerts. *Advances in Economics, Business and Management Research, 15*, 301–308.

Shone, A., & Parry, B. (2010). *Successful Event Management: A Practical Handbook* (3rd ed.). Hampshire: CENGAGE Learning.

Silvers, J. R. (2008). *Risk Management for Meetings and Events*. Oxford: Butterworth Heinemann. doi:10.1016/B978-0-7506-8057-8.50009-2

Tangit, T. M., Kibat, S. A., & Adanan, A. (2016). Lessons in managing visitors experience: The case of future music festival Asia (FMFA) 2014. Malaysia. *Procedia Economics and Finance, 37*, 52–57. doi:10.1016/S2212-5671(16)30092-2

Tarlow, P. E. (2002). *Event Risk Management and Safety*. New York: John Riley & Sons, Inc.

Tum, J., Norton, P., & Wright, N. (2006). *Management of Event Operations*. Oxon: Butterworth-Heinemann.

Upton, M. (2008). *Safe Event Management*. Paper presented at the Theatre Managers Association Conference, Birmingham, UK.

Van der Wagen, L., & White, L. (2006). *Event Management: for tourism, cultural business & sporting events*. Pearson.

Wertheimer, P. L. (1993). *The American Experience: Rock Concert Safety*. Retrieved 20 August 2019 from http://citeseerx.ist.psu.edu/viewdoc/download;jsessionid=E92CF2D29244F3212F22CA626E7F55A6?doi=10.1.1.631.5447&rep=rep1&type=pdf

Wijermanns, N. C., Conrado, M., van Steen, C., Martella, J., & Li, L. (2016). A landscape of crowd-management support: An integrative approach. *Safety Science*, *86*, 142–164. doi:10.1016/j.ssci.2016.02.027

Chapter 5
Understanding and Negotiating Contracts With Venues

Emma Nolan
University of Chichester, UK

ABSTRACT

Signing the venue hire contract is a significant stage in the event planning process as it formalises the agreement with the principal supplier to the event. Venue contracts can be quite lengthy and detailed documents as they cover all aspects of the agreement between the two parties. As well as confirming the hire charges, it will stipulate a number of rules and regulations that will govern the event, and it will outline the penalties for failing to comply with the contract. Much of this is rooted in the venue's plan to ensure that the event complies with relevant legislation and health and safety guidance. This chapter covers the purpose of a venue contract, typical terms and conditions, likely penalties for breaching the contract, plus an overview of venue specific laws and health and safety guidance.

INTRODUCTION

Today event managers can choose from a wide range of venues and open spaces to host their next party, celebration, meeting, wedding, conference or exhibition. Once the location has been selected, signing the venue hire contract becomes a significant stage in the planning process as this is the documentation of the agreement with one of, if not the, principal supplier to the event (Nolan, 2018). Venue contracts can be quite lengthy and detailed documents as they cover all aspects of the agreement

DOI: 10.4018/978-1-7998-3230-0.ch005

between the two parties and the terms and conditions of hire. A contract issued by the venue can be one of the most complex documents of its kind as it can contain a number of specific clauses (Bladen et al, 2012). As well as confirming the hire charges, the contract will stipulate a number of rules and regulations that will govern the event and it will outline the penalties for failing to comply with the contract. Much of this is rooted in the venue's plan to ensure that the event complies with relevant legislation and health and safety guidance. However, hire charges and some terms and conditions can be adjusted before the contract is signed, though a process of negotiation. As Davidson and Hyde confirm 'the key to successful negotiations lies in thorough preparation' (2014, p.61). As such, this chapter provides advice on how to prepare to negotiate with a venue through an exploration of contract terminology, hire charges and the principles of yield management. Once signed, the contract is a legally binding document that will govern how the event will be run and this chapter will also provide an overview of licencing and health and safety guidance and demonstrates how this is embedded in venue contracts.

Understanding Hire Charges

Until the point at which the event manager signs the venue contract, all hire charges and terms and conditions of using the venue are potentially negotiable. Generally, venue hire charges fall into two categories; either a set fee per attendee per day or an hourly charge for each room that is going to be used. A day delegate rate (DDR) is the charge that the venue makes per person attending a specific event, usually a meeting or a one-day conference. The DDR will typically cover the cost of the use of one event room, refreshments (typically lunch and 2 servings of tea and coffee) and a basic AV and stationery package. This charge can often cover all of the event manager's requirements for a meeting, training event or one day conference. For overnight events, a 24-hour rate is usually available if the venue is residential. This charge will everything in the DDR plus an evening meal, one night's accommodation in the venue and breakfast the following morning. For longer or more complex events, where a DDR does not cover all of the event's venue requirements, the venue will provide a detailed quotation which shows the break down of all of the room hire (and additional) charges.

Typically, venues will charge by the hour for the use of each and every room that is going to be used and there is often a minimum hire period of at least 4 hours. Charges are often aligned to the size and therefore the capacity of the room and the bigger the room, the more expensive it will be to use. Similarly, rooms that are already furnished or equipped with facilities such as staging or AV equipment may come at a premium, and this can sometimes be regardless of whether or not the room's equipment and facilities will all be used. The time and date of the event can often determine the charges as many venues, in line with their yield management strategies, will charge more for evening use of the venue and for busy times of the week or year, notably weekends and peak seasons such as national holidays and vacation periods.

The event manager can expect to pay the same hire charge for the get in and get out periods of any event. Furthermore, the venue may apply hire charges to any rooms that are not in constant use during the event but that cannot be hired to another party, for example rooms that have been set up to be used at certain times of the day only. Therefore, the venue may charge for each hour that rooms are essentially being occupied. Additionally, venues can make charges for rooms that have been booked for an event but end up not being used at all and this is called attrition.

Attrition

Attrition (also referred to as slippage) is a term referring to unused room bookings and many venues will include an attrition clause in their hire contract. Essentially this means that if the event manager books rooms for their event that they do not use, they will be charged for them anyway. Such clauses 'provide for the payment of damages to the hotel when a meeting organizer fails to fully utilize the room block specified in the contract' (Fenich, 2012, p.213). Attrition clauses are common in hotel contracts, particularly when accommodation is included in the overall booking. However, they are also used by other types of venues who are adapting similar policies.

Attrition clauses can also be found in contracts that venues have with specific suppliers. For example, some venues will have exclusive providers of certain services (catering, AV, florists etc.) and venues will receive a commission on any income that their exclusive providers make via events taking place at the venue. Therefore, an attrition clause can be imposed if these services are under used by event managers based on the theory that 'the services should be paid for anyway because they were available' (Fenich, 2012, p.60).

Venues may argue that attrition charges are perfectly fair. If the venue manager reserves rooms for an event the event manager does not use them then it is reasonable to expect payment for these rooms. However, some attrition charges can apply even if the event manager alerts the venue to the fact that they no longer require the rooms. The venue may waive attrition charges if they manage to re-hire the rooms to another organisation for a different event. However, if they fail to do this then they are likely to go ahead and impose the full attrition charge. Occasionally some venues will not actively seek to re-let the rooms to another event manager, as they know that they are guaranteed to receive payment from the original booking.

Attrition clauses are commonly used by hotels and other residential venues and they can apply to the booking of accommodation as well as event spaces. This is the case when the event manager has assumed the responsibility of estimating the number of bedrooms that will be required by people attending the event and staying overnight in the venue and booking this accommodation on behalf of these guests. Event managers will often seek to block book accommodation at the venue if it is available as this can mean securing a reduced rate for the event guests. In turn this is an attractive incentive for attending the event. Additionally, residential venues will often offer generous discounts on the hire of event spaces providing that the event manager also books a certain number of bedrooms. This is particularly true if the event is held out of season and some venues will go as far as offering free event space in exchange for the guarantee of the accommodation booking.

However, attrition clauses are often applicable to the booking of bedrooms as well as event spaces and it can be very difficult to accurately estimate the number of people who will want to stay overnight at the venue. Furthermore, many event attendees will use the internet to book accommodation as they may find even cheaper rates online for accommodation at the same venue. This can make attendees feel that the event manager is trying to overcharge them for the accommodation and ultimately will lead them to booking this online and to the attrition clauses being imposed on the event manager.

Therefore, before signing a contract with a venue it is important to check all attrition clauses that relate to the hire of the venue, the booking of bedrooms at the venue and the use of specific suppliers at the venue. Attrition can be avoided with careful event planning and the under-estimation of attendance levels and needs. However, even the most experienced event manager can fall foul of stringent attrition clauses and therefore as part of early negotiations with the venue, it is prudent to ask for all attrition clauses to be lowered or removed entirely from the contract.

Recharges and Penalty Charges

As well as attrition charges, most venues will recharge event managers for a number of items or services provided during the event. These should not come as a surprise as most venues will provide detailed documentation and explanations about additional charges plus the hire contract will also usually indicate the items, services or situations that may incur additional charges. However, as Fenich warns "every square foot of the building has a price attached to it...every chair, every table, and every service provided ...has a price" (2012, p.63). Therefore, the venue may charge for the use of every item of furniture, piece of equipment and electrical socket used as well as any photocopying, printing or other support services provided. Venues may levy charges for staffing an event, which may include providing stewards, cloakroom attendants and security personnel.

A number of event activities are licensable in most countries. This includes the provision of alcohol, gambling and playing of music and licences can usually be obtained to ensure that the activity can be legally conducted at an event. In some cases, the venue will have its own licence which enables the activity to take place on site. But, in lieu of a contribution towards the licence fee, the venue will apply a charge for permitting the licensable activity to go ahead at an event. As with other charges, this should usually be made clear to the event manager well in advance of event day and such charges are usually stated in the venue contract.

As with recharges, venues may apply a number of penalty charges after the event such as an attrition charge. As can be expected, the venue will charge the event manager for any damage to the venue caused at or by the event. This will include any lasting damage left by decorations, activities or any vandalism carried out by anyone at the event. Most venue contracts include a clause which specifically warns about this and therefore the onus is on the event manager to ensure that no damage is caused to the venue. The venue may also impose charges for cleaning, receiving deliveries in advance of the event and for any other 'inconveniences' that they have incurred as a result of hosting an event. However, there are a number of ways of securing the best rates possible for an event through understanding the basic principles of yield management and guaranteeing the venue an income.

Yield Management

Most venue managers use a system of yield management to ensure that they maximise the income derived from room hire. Yield management is "the basic economic theory of supply and demand that dictates that in times of high demand, high prices can be charged, but when demand is low, prices will drop' (Davidson & Rogers, 2016, p.149). In other words, venues will employ strategies to maximise their income by selling their rooms at the best rates possible to ensure that they are filled as much as possible. This means applying different hire charges based on market demands. Yield management is also built upon understanding, predicting and reacting to consumer behaviour (Berger, 2005). This is a technique that was developed by the airline industry and subsequently adopted by hotels, the first venues that began to vary their accommodation rates on a daily basis depending on actual and anticipated demand (Fenich, 2012, p.210).

Today this technique has been adopted and adapted by managers of other types of venues besides hotels. Sporting venues, academic and unusual venues are likely to alter both their day delegate rate and hourly room charges according to the level of demand and rates charged by competitors. These venues, like hotels, are also likely to vary their costs due to the seasonality of the primary function. For example, when a sporting complex is not being used for competitions or training purposes, the hire charges for event space is likely to be at its lowest. This is due to a combination of factors. Firstly, the space is not being used for its primary purpose and therefore any income on rooms that would be otherwise left unused is a bonus to the venue. This can mean that the venue manager may offer very low, competitive rates to encourage bookings to fill the space. Secondly, part of the appeal of holding an event at a sporting venue is to take advantage of the adrenaline filled atmosphere that engulfs a stadium or sports ground on a busy match day. However, this will obviously be lacking on a non-match day and therefore the venue manager may offer lower hire charges to offset the lack of atmosphere. Similarly, a number of unusual venues and academic venues will offer lower hire rates during off peak seasons, particularly when the rooms will be completely unused unless they are sold to event managers.

Yield management is also going to be affected by influences such as changing tastes and interests as well as planned future events, national holidays and unexpected past events such as terrorist attacks (Berger, 2005). A basic understanding of the principles of yield management is key to successfully negotiating with venues, as is guaranteeing the venue an income.

Guaranteeing the Venue Income

Often the best way to secure a discount on venue hire charges, is by ensuring that the venue is still going to make an income from the event and there are several ways to do this.

When using a residential venue, adding accommodation into the booking is a very good way of securing low room hire charges. Lee and Fenich (2016) suggest that a discount could mean securing as much as 40% off of the rack rate (published hire charges). If a significant number of bedrooms will be needed for event guests, this may enable the event manager to negotiate free use of the event space and although this means avoiding potential attrition charges, overall this could mean a significant saving:

Conventional wisdom states that the planners do not pay for meeting space in hotels. However, meeting space costs the hotels money...staff and materials to clean, maintain, and operate the meeting rooms and...these costs must be funded from somewhere. Most often, these costs are covered by requiring the meeting to commit to using a minimum number of sleeping rooms for a minimum number of nights. The hotel's goal is to fill the rooms that would not be filled by its regular customers (Fenich, 2012, p.59).

The same strategy applies to catering as a number of venues have an in house or appointed caterer and in both cases the venue will make an income from the food and drink sold at the event. Therefore, by providing the venue with a guarantee that money will be spent on catering, this can be used to offset the room hire charges. Generally, the only way to provide this guarantee is by agreeing to put at least some of the event catering on account. This is when the catering is paid for by the event manager rather than the event attendees which means that accurately predicting the amount of food and drink that will be required at the event is crucial as the charge will be for the amount of catering ordered, and not the amount that is actually consumed. As with accommodation bookings, this can be a high-risk strategy if the event manager cannot accurately estimate how much food and drink will be required. However, the benefit of being able to predict this, with reasonable accuracy, is that it can be used to offset room hire charges and if an event manager can prebook a significant amount of catering on account this can be used in negotiations as part of a request to waive all room hire charges (Nolan, 2018).

Negotiating with Venues

Booking early can secure the best rates possible as venues are generally keen to have the guarantee of confirmed events as early as possible. Conversely, booking at the last minute can sometimes mean being able to negotiate a very low hire charge because the chances of the venue securing another late booking are slim (Fenich, 2012). However, much of the time the event manager does not have the option of leaving the booking the venue to the last minute as this will hold up the entire event planning process. However, flexibility over the time of year or time of the week when the event is to be held can be used to negotiate the best possible rates. Dates or days of the week that are likely to be unpopular or dates that coincide with when the venue is likely to be quiet increases the chance of securing a discount.

Another way of securing a discount is by understanding the venue layout as if the venue will be unable to hire out certain rooms, they may be inclined to agree to a generous discount on using those rooms. For example, the venue manager is unlikely to hire out any rooms which are beneath or adjacent to rooms that are going to be using for very loud activities (unless they are sound proofed). Any rooms that cannot be accessed without going through a room that is in use are not going to be hired out to other users either. Plus, if an event will be taking up most of the rooms in a venue, leaving one or two small rooms empty, then the venue may struggle to find small enough bookings to fill these rooms. As such it may be possible to secure certain rooms for a substantially reduced hire charge based on their limited usage or appeal to other hirers.

This is an example of how to negotiate with a venue, based on comparing information about the event and about the venue and thinking beyond simply agreed agreeing a price (Davidson & Hyde, 2014). Similarly, an event manager should enter into a negotiation with a view of what they require but also what they can offer the venue in exchange for a discount. Most venues are seeking to forge long term relationships with event managers and in particular they want to be associated with suitable events, work with reliable event managers, make a profit, have repeat bookings and host events that generate an income to their partner organisations. Therefore, when negotiating with venues, event managers should consider what they have to offer in return for a discount. For example, if the event is going to generate media interest, this could this provide the venue with an opportunity to publicize or showcase their facilities. If the event may lead to a rebooking or future booking this could be worth a discount on the hire charges on the current event as a goodwill gesture from the venue. Additionally, if an event manager can demonstrate that they are an experienced and reliable professional and the event is going to be legally compliant, low risk and well organised (and will therefore not take up much of the venue manager's time with lots of questions) this too could be traded for a discount. As such, an understanding of venue legislation and licencing is key to demonstrating professionalism in event production, but also in negotiating contractual terms and conditions.

Venue Legislation and Licensing

Venues will be subject to the general legislation that applies to any business or organisation such as employment, sanitation and public safety laws. In addition, some venues may require a licence or certification in order to operate which also sets the maximum capacity of the venue. For example, in the UK the Safety of Sports Grounds Act 1975 was introduced after the Ibrox Stadium disaster of 1971 when 66 football fans were killed in a crush as they were leaving the venue. Under this act, certain sports venues can only operate if they hold a safety certificate which is issued by the local authority.

All venues must meet the specific health and safety regulations as set down by the national governing authority and these are likely to include laws relating to fire safety and risk assessment. Additionally, venues that are used for events are likely to be subject to specific regulations relating to construction, gaming, special effects and the provision of alcohol to name a few (Quinn, 2013, p.113) and the legislation will usually dictate what is and is not permitted to take place at the venue. A number of typical event activities are often permitted at the venue provided a suitable licence has been sought which many regular event venues will have in place.

Licensable activities can include a number of typical event activities including gambling, the provision of alcohol, the use of children in performances, the playing of music and conducting a civil wedding. Many event venues will have licences in place for activities that take place regularly on site. There may be a charge made to the event manager to conduct the activity at the event, even when the licence is in place, as some venues will expect a contribution towards the cost of the licence fee. Where a licence is not in place, the venue will confirm whether or not the activity is permitted on site. If the venue is in agreement, the event manager can then apply for a specific licence at their own expense. Most licence applications are made through the governing authorities that are local to the venue. The same authorities, or central government, or both, may issue detailed health and safety guidance and legislation relating to the delivery of live events.

Health & Safety Guidance, Legislation and Insurance

In most countries there are basic workplace laws which details the principles for the safe management of premises and people. Additionally, there is usually legislation and guidance related to the control of hazardous substances and the reporting of injuries and incidents such as the UK's Reporting of Injuries, Diseases and Dangerous Occurrences Regulations 2013 (RIDDOR), and the Occupational Safety and Health Acts in Australia and the USA.

Most health and safety legislation ensures that venues conduct a risk assessment of the premises, a fire risk assessment and have a safety policy in place. All of this is part of their responsibilities to their employees as well as other users of the venue such as members of the public and event attendees.

The venue's risk assessment will be a comprehensive review of the premises to include all equipment and facilities on site. The venue may also conduct and record a fire risk assessment which provides a separate review of fire hazards, such as the storage of dangerous substances, and precautions and control measures such as emergency exits, alarms and fire-fighting equipment. The venue's safety policy should detail the emergency and evacuation procedures that are in place at the venue (Raj et al, 2013 p.168) and all of these documents should be available to the event manager on request.

Most venues will have employer insurance in place and in many cases, this will be a legal requirement. Employers are responsible for the wellbeing of their employees while they are at work. Should staff be injured at work or become ill as a result of their job, then they may try to claim compensation from the employer. Employer's liability insurance will help to cover associated costs of such a claim. The owners and managers of public buildings have a similar responsibility to protect the health and safety of their visitors and therefore venues that are open to the public should also have public liability insurance in place. Most venues will insist that every event is covered by a separate public liability insurance policy which will provide financial support in the event of a claim for compensation by anyone who is injured at the event. The venue hire contract will stipulate if the event manager must take out public liability insurance and it is worth remembering that the insurance policy will only be valid if the event manager has also met their responsibilities under the relevant legislation and guidance. As Matthews (2016, p.79) explains further:

Thanks to numerous stage collapses, crowd crushes, fires, and natural disasters at special events around the world in recent years, event liability insurance and often event cancellation insurance have become mandatory in most jurisdictions. Most venues require proof of adequate insurance before they will allow an event to be booked.

Furthermore, venues are also now subject to terrorist attacks and this may lead to the introduction of further legislation in the near future to ensure that venues are adequately prepared for any such incidents (Moritz, 2019). Most venues will ensure that the event manager complies with legislation and guidance and this may become first apparent in the venue hire contract.

Venue Hire Contracts

The key purpose of the contract that the venue will issue to the event manager is to clearly outline in writing the terms and conditions of the booking. The contract is a legal tool used to ensure that both parties, the issuer and the recipient, are aware of their rights and responsibilities with regards to the specific booking. The contract will also include the consequences and penalties of not complying with the agreement. The contract is written in favour of the issuer and it is written to articulate the agreement but also to deter the event manager from acting irresponsibly or ignoring the venue's policies. By detailing the penalties that can be enforced by breaching the contract, the venue is trying to minimise the likelihood of something going wrong, but the contract also protects the venue from the effects of poor event management practices.

For a contact to be legally binding there are 5 key requirements to be met; an offer, acceptance, consideration, intention and capacity.

1. **An Offer:** An offer is the express description of what is being made available. For example, the venue should make reference in the contract to the specific rooms which are available on specific dates to the event manager. The contract should not just list the rooms that are available to hire.
2. **Acceptance**: The contract requires acceptance of the offer. This is usually made in writing, by signing the contract. Normally the venue will make it clear to the event manager what kind of acceptance they require such as agreement via email. Acceptance applies to the whole offer and it cannot apply to part of it.

This means that the event manager should not sign the contract until they are happy to accept every detail of the agreement. The venue cannot assume that silence indicates acceptance, for example, the venue cannot say to the event manager that they will assume the contract has been agreed if they do not hear otherwise.

3. **Consideration:** Consideration refers to what will be exchanged between the two parties in order to seal the agreement. This can usually be measured in economic terms such as the provision of money in exchange for goods or services. Therefore, the venue contract will normally indicate the hire charges that apply to the specific booking.
4. **Intention**: Intention refers to the notion that the two parties mean to create the agreement and enter into the agreement purposefully.
5. **Capacity**: Capacity means that both parties must have the capacity to enter into the contract. For example, children cannot enter into legally binding contracts. This means that both the issuer, the venue, and the recipient, the event manager must have the capacity to sign the contract. For event managers, this means accepting responsibility for the event that is being organised (as opposed to the client accepting responsibility). The venue manager cannot offer the event manager the use of rooms that they do not own and operate, and the event manager cannot sign if they do not have the authority (e.g. from the client) to enter into the agreement.

In order to ensure that the contract is a legally binding document it should be written by a qualified professional and the event manager should get a similarly qualified person to read it before they sign it.

Every venue will have their own format for contracts and hirers can expect to receive a bespoke contract which has been personalised to cover their specific event requirements. There are a number of typical entries on any venue hire contract to include what the venue is providing and the terms and conditions of hire. Some of the most common entries include the name and address of the venue, the contact information for the venue including the name of at least one member of staff. The name of the event, or reference to the type of event or client should be noted as well as the name and contact details of the event manager. The names of each of the rooms that are being hired should be listed on the contract and against each the dates and times of usage to include the get in and get out periods. The contract may detail the agreed room set ups and timings of the event. Although frequently the contract is issued before the event manager is in a position to confirm all of these details. Therefore, it is quite common for this to be agreed and noted via a function sheet or operational schedule much later although it can be useful if the contract indicates how and when the venue expects to document these arrangements. The contract may list the equipment and services to be provided by the venue, but these may also be added to later documentation.

The contact will specify the venue's rules regarding catering, AV, staffing and stewarding. For example, the contract will indicate if the hirer is obliged to use the venue's own teams and equipment or may choose from a list of preferred suppliers. If the venue is going to provide security, stewarding or technical support staff the contract should itemise the hourly charges and the minimum work period (e.g. staff work for a minimum of 4 hours). The contract will refer to what is permitted in terms of signage and decoration and will include details of the penalties for damaging the venue. For events such as exhibitions and shows, the venue will specify any particular rules concerning loading and unloading, the installation of infrastructure and the collection of rubbish during the event. Frequently the contract will specify the terms of the licences in place and indicate the nature of licensable activities that may be permitted but that will require the event manager to first secure a valid licence.

It is not uncommon for the venue contract to stipulate that all event marketing materials must be approved by the venue manager before it is to be used and the process for this may be included in the contract. The contact will also refer to the health and safety obligations of the event manager and the venue hire contract may make it clear that the venue manager must approve the event risk assessment and operational schedule and receive a copy of the public liability insurance cover.

Furthermore, as Silvers (2013, p.58) indicates, the contract may reference a number of very specific rules such as the:

legal restrictions on what types of special effects are allowed, the construction of temporary structures such as grandstands or viewing platforms, and where smoking may and may not be allowed. There may be venue restrictions on what signage may or must be posted or what sponsor banners may be displayed, which food providers may be used, and which workers are allowed to perform what tasks. There may be specifications on how loud or late music may be played, how many portable toilets must be provided, and where guests are allowed to park.

The venue contract may also make reference to what is available in terms of car parking, storage, access for loading and unloading, options for recording the event, details of first aid provision, cloakroom facilities etc. Finally, the contact should include detailed financial information including the room hire charges, the arrangement for paying a deposit and balance and details of the charges for services or equipment to be provided by the venue. The contract will also make reference to the penalties that will be imposed should any aspect of the contract be broken, and this may extend to what will happen if the venue breaches the contract.

Avoiding a Breach of Contract

Venue contracts can be long, complex and detailed documents. Reading through a contract can be baffling and overwhelming and therefore it is extremely important to seek professional advice before signing a contract. However, the first step towards understanding the contract is recognising that it is used by the venue to protect their organisation and to mitigate against the poor management of events. Much of the content of the contract, although written using punitive language, is to encourage the organiser to act responsibly in the management of their event (Nolan, 2018).

In the eyes of the law, it can be difficult to identify which party is responsible for the safe delivery of the event; the venue or the event manager. As such the contract may make explicit references to the event manager's responsibility for complying with legislation relating to copyright, licencing, the provision of music, alcohol and staff.

As the multitude of preventable event disasters over recent years indicate that the greatest risk to human life at events are caused by fire, overcrowding or infrastructure collapse, the venue may take much responsibility for minimising risks in these areas notably by conducting an annual fire risk assessment and dictating the room capacities. The venue may also insist on providing their own event staff and approving a number of event documents as part of their responsibility towards minimising the risk of overcrowding and fires. They may want to approve the event operational schedule, which details all of the event activities, for this reason. This is sometimes referred to as a production or event schedule and it is a detailed timetable covering the whole duration of the event. The venue may want to review the event risk assessment and some venues will insist that the risk assessment is conducted via a specific template. Additionally, the local authorities may also insist on approving plans for installing temporary structures within the venue, such as a shell scheme exhibition. The purpose of reviewing, possibly amending, and ultimately approving event documentation is not to control the event or to find ways to extract more money from the event manager, but to check for early indications of preventable risks.

The venue may insist that they receive copies of riders and technical riders from any performers attending the event. As much of the content of the rider will need to be provided by the venue, this is another safeguarding measure to establish if the venue are able to meet the requirements of the artists and to flag up any additional costs the event manager may incur as a result of the agreement. Similarly, the venue may insist upon reviewing the risk assessments of third-party suppliers that the event manager will be hiring to work at the event. Once again this is to alert the venue to any possible problems and so that the venue can be assured that all event staff will be adhering to safe work practices. This is also to ensure that the venue's own insurance policies are not rendered void. Raj *et al* (2013, p.300) illustrates this further:

If an event is held within a venue which has the structure to allow working at height, the venue manager should insist that persons wear a harness when working above head height. Again, if this procedure is not adhered to the venue insurance cover could be invalidated, along with the insurance cover held by the production company.

The venue contract should make the financial arrangement for the hire of the rooms very clear. Typically, this means that the hirer is required to pay a deposit in advance of the event, and often this is payable at the time of booking and singing the contract. The deposit may or may not be refundable and the conditions for this should also be included in the contract. If the event manager is now known to the venue, then it is possible that the venue manager will insist upon full payment in advance of the event. This is sometimes included to deter amateur event managers from making bookings for events that they are not capable of delivering. Ultimately these clauses ensure that the venue does not make a significant financial loss by accepting the booking and blocking out the use of the venue to other interested parties. The catering requirements will usually be included in the contract if the caterer is in house or appointed. As with the room hire charges, a deposit may be required well in advance of event day. Often, the full catering charges must be paid in advance of the event and the contract will normally determine the dates by which the catering numbers must be confirmed to the venue. After this date, it may not be possible to make any changes to these numbers, but it is particularly unlikely that a refund will be available should the catering numbers go down. This is because the caterer will need to pre-order food and drink, and much of this will be perishable.

All of the financial payments listed on the contract should also make reference to applicable local taxes, such as VAT, and indicate whether the figures shown are net or gross. In some countries, the government may refund certain taxes upon proof of payment and this information should be clearly evident on the contract (Matthews, 2016).

The contract should clearly detail all of the penalties that apply to both parties (venue and event manager) should either party breach any part of the agreement. A breach of contract can occur when either party fail to fulfil any of their responsibilities listed on the contract or undertake actions which go against the intent of the contract. Typically, the penalties come in the form of financial charges to either reimburse or compensate the injured party. Cancellation charges should be evident, and most venues apply a sliding scale of charges. This means that should the event manager cancel the event; the imposed charges will be greater the nearer this happens to the event date. The same may apply to the catering charges. The contract should also indicate what will happen should the venue cancel the booking.

The contract should include full details of specific costs, such as room hire charges, and estimated costs of variable items such as furniture, equipment, staffing etc. Any attrition charges should be detailed, listing the charges for the minimum number of accommodation bookings, even if the bedrooms are not occupied. Some venues apply a fine for when the event overruns and you can expect to be charged for any damage done to the venue at any time during the event (including get in and get out periods).

Force majeure (French for 'superior force') is a clause which permits either party to suspend or terminate the contract in the event of circumstances beyond their control. This include acts of God (e.g. flood, hurricane etc.), war, mass public outcry (e.g. riots, strikes), explosions and government actions. And finally, the contract may include an indemnity or limitation of liability clause. Essentially this clarifies that the event manager assumes all responsibility for the management of the event and thus it protects the venue from any associated harm, loss or responsibility.

The Venue's Contractual Responsibilities

Although the contract is primarily designed to protect the interests of the venue, as a legally binding document it also protects the event manager. The contract will stipulate which rooms are going to be provided, on what dates and at what hire charge. It may also list all of the furniture, services and equipment that the venue will either provide or arrange and also at what cost. Although the charges may rise annually in line with inflation (and if so, this should be indicated in the document) the contract provides the event manager with a clear list of charges. Although some will be variable, and dependent on numbers for example, the contract provides the event manager with the means to financially predict and control the event budget and as such it is a useful planning tool. The contract, once signed by both parties, confirms that the booking has been agreed. This should mean that the venue does not offer the same rooms and facilities to another user. Unfortunately, the contract does not provide a cast iron guarantee that the venue will not double book the space. However, it does reduce the likelihood of this occurring and ensures that should the venue make such an error, the event manager will be financially compensated.

The contract also provides the event manager with a useful checklist of what the venue has agreed to provide and what you must arrange yourself. The list of documents that must be provided to the venue, and the payment schedule, are also useful planning tools which enable the event manager to effectively manage the event. Approval from the venue manager of documents such as risk assessments, is a mechanism for getting valuable feedback from an industry professional.

The contract may also refer to the location of the venue, as there may be a number of laws directly applicable to the management of buildings, as Davidson and Rogers (2011, p.40) illustrate:

Much of the activity in the area of accessibility is at the level of the individual event venue. Venus are encouraged as a matter of best practice, and required, by legislation, to provide appropriate signage, meeting space, bedrooms, equipment to ensure full accessibility for those with disabilities.

And as Raj *et al* (2013) remind us, the event manager has a duty to check that the venue has all of their documentation in place and is meeting their legal requirements.

Transferring Responsibility to Suppliers and Attendees

Although the contract will become a legally binding document, once signed, the terms and conditions of the contract can be negotiated and altered until both parties are content with the final agreement. Upon receipt of the contract, it is wise to get a professional to look check the wording of the agreement and to flag up any concerning clauses or penalties or clarify any clauses that are not completely clear. It is also an opportunity to add to the contract. For example, Fenich (2012, p.199) reminds us that "everything is negotiable" and Bladen *et al* (2012, p.88) suggest that the point of signing the contract should be viewed as an opportunity to negotiate rates and charges once again. The contract can be amended after it has been signed and frequently the event manager will need to add to or alter details as the event plans develop. However, your bargaining powers are reduced once you have entered into a legal agreement with the venue, or indeed with any event supplier and as such event managers must consider how to transfer responsibility to suppliers and event attendees.

One of the fundamental roles of the contract is to set out the obligations of both parties, but also to transfer responsibility from venue to event owner. As previously stated, the contract may include a number of punitive statements, but generally these are used to encourage the event owner to act responsibly in the management of their event. Part of acting responsible involves understanding the venue's procedures and policies and relaying them to event guests and other event suppliers as appropriate. As Raj *et al* (2013, p.168) illustrate:

The event company has a legal responsibility to relay the health and safety and evacuation procedures presented by the venue to all employees of the event company, suppliers or outside contractual staff working within the venue. This information must be presented and understood prior to any outside employee commencing work within the venue.

It is important to ensure that event suppliers also act responsibly at the event, partly to ensure that the event manager is complying with the terms and conditions of the contract. This means that much information must be conveyed to suppliers to ensure that they work within the venue's policies and provide the event manager with information that must be passed on to the venue. This may include plans for installations of temporary structures, risk assessments for all activities and services to be provided at events, copies of public liability insurance from all suppliers, riders from performers and the technical requirements of all suppliers. This needs to be done in a timely manner, as some contracts will include details fines for the late provision of information to the venue.

Additionally, event managers will need to ensure that attendees comply with venue policies and rules and this will involve going through the contract to draw out any clauses that could be broken by event guests. Typically, this can include damaging the venue, smoking where it is prohibited and bringing food and drink on site rather than purchasing it from the caterer. Event managers must promote responsible behaviour in guests well in advance of the event, through means such as establishing event rules and policies. Behaviour must also be monitored on event day to ensure that the event manager does not incur any penalty charges for breaking the venue's rules, as outlined in the contract.

CONCLUSION

The contract issued by a venue to the event owner is one of the most complicated types of contract as it is likely to contain a number of specific clauses (Bladen *et al*, 2012). Therefore, it is essential that event managers understand the key terms used in these documents as contracts play a vital role in event management (Goldblatt, 2007). It is therefore important to read the contract carefully and involve the services of a legal professional before signing it. Any final negotiating with the venue should be conducted prior to (and as part of) the process of signing the contract.

The contract will make reference to specific legislation, policies and rules that apply to the particular booking. It will also outline the payment plan for the hire of the venue and give details of the penalties in place for not meeting the terms and conditions of the contract. The contract will also confirm the responsibilities of the venue and it will be signed by the venue manager. The contract can provide the event manager with a useful checklist of information that must be collected and shared with the venue as well as rules that must be upheld on event day. Well trained event staff can help the event manager to comply with the contract by monitoring the activities of suppliers and guests while at the venue and upholding the venue's and the event's policies. Signing the venue hire contract is a significant stage in the event planning process as it signals confirmation of the event date and therefore a commitment to delivering the event and finalising the event plans. Therefore, once the contract has been received, read and signed the relationship between the event manager and the venue enters into a new and important phase.

REFERENCES

BergerJ. (2005). *Profiting with Yield Pricing*. Retrieved from: Http://Www.Wiglafjournal.Com/Pricing/2005/12/Profiting-With-Yield-Pricing

Bladen, C., Kennell, J., Abson, E., & Wilde, N. (2012). *Events Management: An Introduction*. Abingdon: Routledge. doi:10.4324/9780203852972

Boh, M. (2019). *The Rise of the Hybrid Venue*. Retrieved from: https://www.conference-news.co.uk/blogs/rise-hybrid-venue

Davidson, R., & Hyde, A. (2014). *Winning Meetings and Events for Your Venue*. Oxford: Goodfellow.

Davidson, R., & Rogers, T. (2016). *Marketing Destinations and Venues for Conferences, Conventions and Business Events* (2nd ed.). Abingdon: Routledge.

Edwards, D., Foley, C., Dwyer, L., Schlenker, K., & Hergesell, A. (2014). Evaluating the Economic Contribution of a Large Indoor Entertainment Venue: An Inscope Expenditure Study. *Event Management*, *18*(4), 407–420. doi:10.3727/152599514X14143427352076

Fenich, G. (2012). Meetings, Expositions, Events, And Conferences: An Introduction to The Industry (3rd ed.). Pearson.

Fullard, M. (2019). *Preferential Treatment*. Retrieved from https://www.conference-news.co.uk/blogs/preferential-treatment

Goldblatt, J. (2007). *Special Events: The Roots and Wings of Celebration* (5th ed.). New York: Wiley.

Lee, S., & Fenich, G. (2016). Perceived Fairness of Room Blocks in the Meetings, Incentives, Convention, and Exhibition Industry. *Journal of Convention & Event Tourism*, *17*(2), 159–171. doi:10.1080/15470148.2016.1171187

Matthews, D. (2016). *Special Event Production: The Process* (2nd ed.). Abingdon: Routledge.

Moritz, J. (2019). *Venues 'still too vulnerable to attack'*. Retrieved from: https://www.mast-security.com/blog/mast-general-news/venues-still-vulnerable-to-attack/

Nolan, E. (2018). *Working with Venues on Events*. London: Routledge.

Quinn, B. (2013). *Key Concepts in Event Management*. London: SAGE. doi:10.4135/9781473914742

Raj, R., Walters, P., & Rashid, T. (2013). *Events Management: Principles and Practice* (2nd ed.). London: SAGE.

Rogers, T. (2013). *Conferences and Conventions: A Global Industry* (3rd ed.). Abingdon: Routledge. doi:10.4324/9780203119402

Silvers, J. R. (2013). *Risk Management for Meetings and Events*. Abingdon: Routledge.

ADDITIONAL READING

Becker, D. (2006). *The Essential Legal Guide to Events: A Practical Handbook for Event Professionals and Their Advisors. Publisher*. Author.

Davidson, R., & Hyde, A. (2014). *Winning Meetings and Events for Your Venue*. Oxford: Goodfellow.

Fenich, G. (2012). *Meetings, Expositions, Events, and Conferences: An Introduction to The Industry* (3rd ed.). Pearson.

Lee, S., & Fenich, G. (2016). Perceived Fairness of Room Blocks in the Meetings, Incentives, Convention, and Exhibition Industry. *Journal of Convention & Event Tourism, 17*(2), 159–171. doi:10.1080/15470148.2016.1171187

Nolan, E. (2018). *Working with Venues on Events*. London: Routledge.

Silvers, J. R, (2013). *Risk Management for Meetings and Events*. Abingdon: Routledge.

Tarlow, P. E. (2002). *Event Risk Management and Safety*. New York: Wiley.

Van Der Wagen, L. (2014). *Human Resource Management for Events* (2nd ed.). Abingdon: Routledge.

Chapter 6
Event Management and Terrorism in a Global Order:
A Preliminary Insight

Maximiliano Emanuel Korstanje
University of Palermo, Buenos Aires, Argentina

ABSTRACT

Over the recent years, the public spectacle and media events have become fertile grounds for terrorist attacks. Particularly, media events play a leading role enhancing the social cohesion as well as revitalizing the psychological frustrations that happened during the working days. Paradoxically, terrorism needs to maximize its gains while the costs are minimized. The spectacularisation tourism and events offer a double-edge sword. The same attractiveness that makes global cities a safer place to live are employed by the terrorist cells to cause chaos and uncertainty. The chapter theoretically explores the difficult interrelation between terrorism and event management as well as the conceptual limitations of Western rationality to understand the "undesired Other."

INTRODUCTION

It is noteworthy that a chapter about terrorism should start with a clear and coherent definition of the term. Here the problem seems to be that there is a great dispersion of the produced knowledge, as well as the lack of a shared epistemology to study terrorism (Stampnitzky, 2013; McCauley & Moskalenko, 2014). Each discipline and the different authors worked and developed different definitions on the phenomenon. As Marc Sageman puts it, terrorism research faces a facet of stagnation and

DOI: 10.4018/978-1-7998-3230-0.ch006

conceptual fragmentation as never before. In spite of the several volumes, books and updating of the bibliographical literature, today scholars are unable to answer furtherly on the objective conditions that finally lead a good person to become in a terrorist. Part of the problem comes from the interventions of governments and the intelligence community to fund the main borders of the produced research. In other words, Government agencies invested their own financial resources so that the intellectuals reaffirm their own preconceptions about terrorism. Concerned on the necessary good practices to protect us from terrorism than in understanding terrorism as a complex socio-political phenomenon, the advances in the fields ushered the academia to misleading outcomes. In his book Witnessing Terror, Australian sociologist Luke Howie calls the attention on the role performed by the media inviting to "pseudo-scholars" to talk about terrorism. This happens because terrorism is an extremely-centred illegal activity which is considered a serious crime against the state. Those ethnographers, who are narrowly in contact with terrorist cells, are fiercely pressed to reveal their key-informants. Hence it is hard to study terrorism in a society that condemns it. What is clear is that terrorists do not look a lot of people dying they want a lot of people watching. Howie (2012) reminds not only the leading role of the mass-media creating pseudo-events –a term coined by Baudrillard, but also in disseminating fear as a form of cultural entertainment. In so doing terrorists look to create political instability in order for their claims to be unilaterally accepted. The attacks against the World Trade Center and the Pentagon were more than social tragedies. Both represented the humiliation of the West and the commoditization of the death in the same media stage. Methodologically speaking, ethnographers should study terrorism by its direct effects in society and day-to-day life. Otherwise, they fall in mere speculations.

As the previous backdrop, no less true seems to be that 9/11 marked a new epoch not only for the geopolitical relationships but also a novel tactic where innocent travellers as tourists and journalists are killed. Terrorists, echoing Enders & Sandler (2011), are far from irrational maniacs who kill for pleasure. They carefully select leisure-hot spots and tourist destinations because the attack has durable effects. Terrorists tactically move to maximize their gains while minimizing the costs. They are not irrational killers or hatred-filled maniacs. Their targets are selected according to a specific semiotic message to transmit. The tourism industry not only is vulnerable to terrorism but also offers the perfect ground to give a lesson to the world: anyone and anytime can be a victim of terrorism. The flexibility of tourist resorts in allowing the passengers traffic, as well as the resistance of tourists to be close of military forces makes of hotels and tourist destination an easy target for terrorism. Besides, the psychological impacts of watching corpses mutilated through spaces designed to pleasure and leisure materializes high-levels of fear and anxiety. Since the tourist destinations are public spaces, lay-people believe that they would be a potential victim of terrorism at a later day. This affects seriously the economy of the tourism industry in some peripheral economies. In this way, policy-makers and experts of all stripes have agreed that terrorism exhibits a major danger for the tourism industry worldwide (Richter & Waugh 2986; Somnez 1998; Arana & Leon 2008; Tarlow 2014).

Having said this, no less true is that tourism and event-management have notably evolved as promising industries over the recent years attracting not only foreign investment but also the attention of radicalized cells. Taylor & Toohey (2005) suggest that the post 9/11 contexts witnessed not only the increase of security costs while organizing media events but also a substantial shift in the stakeholder expectations. Three years after 9/11, Australia held two major events, the Rugby World Cup and the Olympic Games. The consumers´ expectances are notably influenced by terrorism and the priorities to attend to a safe event. Still further, the Australian social imaginary was shocked after the attacks in Bali where 88 Australian tourists were assassinated. Authors want to understand how the sense of security is culturally fabricated but individually negotiated or internalized. Their findings indicate the following axioms. Although the security costs have risen, attendants to Rugby World Cup (RWC) do not feel Sydney was an insecure destination. This delineates a subtle border between leisure travellers and sports tourists. As Enrico Quarantelli brilliantly observed, the process of perception is in some occasions dissociated from the subject´s cognitive system. While attending to a football game in Los Angeles, the earthquake which whipped the city in the 80s decade remains imperceptible for the attendants. Visibility and perception play a leading role in the configuration of security-related programs in the fields of event management (Quarantelli 2005).

The present chapter explores the limitations and challenges of the specialized literature in the years to come, laying the foundations to a new paradigm to understand security and safety in event management. Here two significant questions arise: is terrorism a direct result of globalization?, and are terrorists in quest of instant visibility for their political demand to be heart?

Terrorism and the Global Audience

The "scourge of terrorism", at least as it was symbolically baptized by the authorities in the US and Europe, has been widely studied by different academic waves. From the left to the right-wing, scholars have focused their attention on terrorism and its effects in daily life (Pipes 1986; Sylas 2006). While a bunch of writers strongly believe that terrorism is a major threat for the western democracies and the economic prosperity (Huntington 2002; Keohane 2005; Keohane & Zeckhauser, 2003; Kepel 2017), other voices alert on the problems the counter-terrorism measure engender (Altheide 2004; Skoll 2010; Chomsky 2015). The former signals to the urgency to eradicate terrorism through the articulation of modern algorithm models as well as the surveillance-related technology whereas the latter refers to the negative effects the process of securitization, which asks for further security, entails for the democratic institutions (Altheide 2017). Quite aside from this polemic, as Luke Howie brilliantly noted, terrorism is an extremely illegal activity which is heavily punished by the state (considered often an act of cowardice). In consequence, for the good fieldworkers, it is very hard to get the first source information or interview of a terrorist leader. Methodologically speaking, fieldworkers not only are restricted to conduct their research but also often pressed to reveal the identity of the key-informants. The gap enlarged by the ethical condemnation of terrorist crimes and the populist process of securitization is finally filled by the media and "the pseudo-experts" who are paid to validate the dominant discourse of the status quo (Howie 2012). The symbiosis between media and terrorism has durable effects on the collective psyche (Hoskins & O´Loughling 2007) affecting sometimes not only the public opinion but also the governance of society. In a seminal book, which entitles *Disciplining Terror*, Lisa Stampnitzky (2013) calls attention on the evolution and maturation of the specialized literature in terrorism fields. While in its infancy, the literature –through the 70s decade- suggested that terrorism would be understood as a clash of asymmetrical powers. More associated with the guerrilla, after all, terrorists targeted celebrities and chief police officers. At the time terrorism target innocent civilians (i.e Al-Qaeda or ISIS) a moral imprint was gradually imposed to the Academia moulding and affecting the content of the produced knowledge. Despite the efforts of academicians and financial support, today terrorism remains still as an act of evil which needs to be eradicated. As Stampnitzky acknowledges, by adopting a moral definition of terrorism obscures more than it clarifies. The paradox lies in the fact while moving forward a more maturated stage of production, terrorism-related studies became more partisan. From the same premise starts Mahmoud Eid (2014), Professor at the University of Toronto, in his book Exchanging Terrorism oxygen for media airwaves. In his text, Eid introduces the term Terroredia, a neologism oriented to denote a strange interlink between media and terror. He toys with the belief that not only terrorists have fluency in English they employ the same digital technology, as well as the rationality, of the West. They are even familiarized of Facebook, Twitter and other social networks. We, the westerners, are shocked but at the same time fascinated by terrorism. To wit, terrorists employ the digital media in order to make their attacks public reaching –in this way- to a wider audience. Needless to say that there is a dependency on journalism (media) and terrorism, as Eid notes. The needs of gaining further advertising, profits or financial funds lead very well to media to cover the terrorist attacks in detail. What is equally important, terrorists need their message to be rapidly and widely disseminated. This creates a dangerous symbiosis Eid baptized as "Terroredia" (Eid 2014: 222)

"In terms of media coverage of protest movements, we could expect ruling class interests to include maintaining the status quo, and therefore, efforts to marginalize dissent and dissenters attempts to make them seem deviant and strange. Likewise, American Middle East foreign policy has long been criticized for the tendency to support corrupt autocratic dictators friendly to elite capitalists (particularly oil companies)". (p. 222)

As this backdrop, Eid argues that terrorism situated as something more complex than a global threat, it rather represents a "global commodity" which is packaged, sold and exchanged by the mass media. The postmodern politics administer resources to struggling against "an invisible enemy". The War on Terror, declared by Bush´s administration, is conducive with such an end. The current obsession in defeating terrorism, associated with the inefficacy in counter-terrorism tactics, is gradually ushering the US into a climate of uncertainty and fear. In order for surviving, terrorists look to gain public attention through the lens of mass media but at the same time, the media is receptive of terrorism-led news. The terror acts as the necessary oxygen of some radicalized groups and media corporations which operate globally in order for the audience to be passively domesticated (Eid 2014).

Last but not least, L. Howie (2018) in Terrorism, the Worker and the City obtains similarly-based results. Taking his cue from Baudrillard, Howie contends that terrorism, in fact, moves to create real effects in real life. Terrorists do not want a lot of people dying, as the literature imagines, rather they want a lot of people watching. Although terrorism appears not to be new, because it is traceable to ancient times, no less true is that the digital media have recreated the borders of a new flat earth (screen) where news is covered and disseminated 24/7 to wider spectatorship. The sentiment of terror instilled by the media not only takes a durable effect but also gravitates furtherly on those countries –like Australia- geographically far away from the operation centres. Terrorism indeed is felt when nothing really explodes. To put this in other terms, people living in New York or LA are sensitive to terrorism because of their tragic legacy, but Australians have nothing experienced a direct attack in their soil. Howie shows how the process of witnessing (which makes the terrorist attacks public) are stronger in the periphery than in the centre.

"I explore the meaning of human security, precariousness and vulnerability in organizational, managerial, city-dwelling and workplace settings. Working people, particularly those in major cities, have been preferred targets for contemporary terrorism. Life in the city has perhaps always been risky, but the post 9/11, post-Madrid, post 7/7 city is filled with witnesses and victims of terrorism going about their work and lives in routine, mundane and everyday ways – I argue that is the essence of terror-work" (Howie 2018: p. 14)

He holds polemically that terrorism does not harm business but inversely it surfaces as a new type of business and amassing profits. Terrorism derives from an innermost emotion, fear and we cannot struggle against fear. Hence, the War on Terror is doomed to fail. The same applies to the process of securitization and the populist demands of further security. We devote our efforts to making the home a safer place, and of course, we can do it. But fear is an emotion. No matter how secure our society is, our fears can be politically manipulated when the opportunity arises. Howie goes on to write,

"I set out in this book to show how contemporary terrorism has consequences for working people and businesses in contemporary cities. I also wanted to show how terrorism transcends the time and space in which it first occurred –the flashpoint- in order for it be reanimated as an image over and over again. In this way, the Twin Tower continue to fall and trains and buses continue to explode in the minds of the world´s workers… I hope to demonstrate here that terrorism does not occur when there are death and destruction –this is violence- but where witness terrorism as a simulation, an image and a spectacle. In short, terrorism exists where terror is felt (p 164).

The question of whether Howie is right, reveals two important implicit assumptions. On one hand, terrorism works hard in order for its crimes to see the light of publicity. In doing so, they target leisure hot spots and tourist destinations. To some extent, they are not familiar with the victims whose lives they take. Tourists are instrumentalized (if not cannibalized) to achieve certain goals. There is a clear process of depersonalization in the planning of attacks. On another, festivals, media events, sporting games (to name a few) represent fertile grounds for radicalized cells. The efforts of policy-makers, as well as marketing experts who devote time in the design of safe venues, evaporate in seconds just after an attack takes hit. The bad advertising wreaks havoc in the necessary trust that needs the tourism industry to survive (Ryan 1993; Mawby 2000; Hall, Timohty & Duval 2004).

Event Management and Terrorism

Events and Festivals are significant social facts disposed to enhance the social cohesion. To set an example, the Olympic Games were mainly organized in Ancient Greece not only to avoid real disputes and warfare among the Greek cities but also as a form of cultural production. The political hierarchies, as well as social institutions, were certainly cemented through the celebrations of games which were peaceful substitutes of war. Those warriors who won more competences and medals have a further reputation which was systematically endorsed to the cities where they came (Spivey 2005). Event management, echoing Dayan & Katz (1994), fabricates and transmits complex cultural codes which are organized to give a message to the spectators and attendants. These events provide exceptional things to think about, suspending the humdrum routine. As a rite of passage which needs to be perfectly articulated, any problem, conflict or discrepancy should be rapidly resolved. If not, the authorities face a lack of credibility and legitimacy. To some extent, it is important not to lose sight of the fact that some radicalized groups target these types of events in order to create political instability (Toohey & Taylor 2008). One of the most famous events that shocked the world was the Munich Massacre in 1972. At this instance, the Palestinian group Black September hosted and killed eleven Olympic team members, who lodged in Munich in order to compete in the Summer Olympic Games. The Boston Marathon bombing whipped the US on 15 April of 2013 while other similar attacks happened worldwide. As Toohey & Taylor (2008) put it, though the attacks on events and games are uncanny, in fact, because the financial efforts in the fields of safety and security, no less true is that its symbolic effects are devastating. For some reason, terrorists look to harming athletes in games in view of immense attention these types of events generate. Terrorists carefully plan their attacks by gaining much exposure as possible. Hence, mega-events, music festivals and other similarly-based events are fertile grounds for their attacks. Peter Tarlow (2014) argues convincingly that the social imaginary toys with the belief of risk-zero society but this is an impossible dream. Security interrogates on the philosophical existence of the man, and it is impossible to achieve a risk-zero atmosphere. While events are anthropologically speaking rites of passage oriented to undermine the levels of anxieties in the society, terrorist radicalized cells want the contrary. In his new book Sports Travel Security, Tarlow (2017) debates the misleading dichotomies between the idealization of sports and emotions. Not surprisingly, the athletic games are complex rites which escape to the simple forms of entertainment. Games not only attract thousands of visitors but also cultivate human skills and relationships. The figure of spectatorship plays a crucial role in the formation of social ties. For some reason which is very hard to precise here, the specialized literature has historically ignored the position of athletes and the symbolic archetype revolving around them. The notion of security, for this reason, is of paramount importance and should be widely considered a priority of governments. Tarlow goes on to write

"In this way, many athletes not only are objectified but also they appear more often in the media. This means that their private lives are often not their own, and their notoriety exposes them to unscrupulous people". (Tarlow 2017, 6)

The security programs orchestrated by the specialists should take attention to the protection of athletes as well as the environmental background of the venue, the city or the infrastructure designed to the security issues. Sometimes, while international disputes –to set an example among the states- leads often to a climate of hostility against a certain nationality or in others athletes´ security is seriously compromised by the lack of civil warranties in the hosting society (Tarlow 2017).

It is interesting to discuss to what extent mega-events are a fertile source of terrorism. Terrorism introduces a message in society aimed at undermining states or creating political instability. From immemorial times, human beings have managed festivals and mega-events not only to celebrate a good harvest but also to strengthen the social bond. Mediated events are, at least, significant celebrations that contribute socially to the reproduction of society. In view of this, some groups which are antagonistic to the state, attack attendees at the events as a way to create panic, undermining not only the legitimacy of the government but the trust of citizens in their institutions. This double effect has been widely studied by sociologists and anthropologists in terrorism-related issues. However, less attention has been given to the fact that leisure spaces are preferred by terrorists to plan their acts. This raises an interesting point of debate based on the connection between terrorism, leisure, and mega-events that deserves to be continued, what is terrorism? What terrorists opt to target festivals and events? Is the nation-state able to prevent the next attack? Why does leisure represent a fertile source of terrorism?

Dayan and Katz (1994) explain that media events are important to improve the mechanisms of reinforcement and reproduction of societies. While the former signals to the sources to legitimate the officialdom´s authority the latter refers to the cultural values -shared by all citizens- that determine the social institutions. Following this, most of the message in these spectacles corresponds with the legitimating of elites and assurance of a broader national being. If some rebellious groups want to cause psychological distress in the community, these types of events offer a particularly fertile space to inflict damage to society. In this respect, the present chapter explored critically the semiotic contours of terrorism in order for readers to expand their current understanding of this deep-seated issue. Doubtless, the connection between terrorism and event management reminds us of the roots of hospitality. The act of perpetrating a terrorist attack in the middle of a mega-event equates to killing the guest while they are sleeping. The hosting country seems to be ethically responsible for the security of attendants, as well as for the evolution of the game. It is important to realise not all risks have the same effect in society. Those risks or hazards, which threaten the principle which hospitality event management emulates, resonate higher than others like local crime. Even though local crime places the security of tourists in jeopardy, terrorism appeals to mining the credibility of the state before other states and their own citizens as a major threat. After all, successful acts of terrorism remind us that when the state is hand-tied to protect strangers it will be unable to protect its own citizens.

Legal Implication of Event Management

In a hyper-globalized world, tourists not only are travellers they are real ambassadors of their nations. Terrorism knows this and often kill foreign tourists to create geopolitical disputes. Just after the days, Bali was targeted, Australia pressed Malaysia to give a formal explanation about the incident. While some countries can be blamed for supporting financially terrorist cells, others build international alliances to intervene or change the geopolitical relationships (Coleman 2003). Doubtless, terrorism creates paradoxical situations in the international legal background (Epifanio 2011). Although defined as an illegal activity, there is a political vacuum regarding the international laws and the jurisprudence which may be used or evoked to struggle against terrorism worldwide. It is important not to lose the sight of the fact that though crime is internationally defined as a crime, each state –in the international laws- have faculties and independence to declare what is punishable or not. Some cases like inter-state aggression or genocides are often labelled as international crimes, as Schmid adheres but terrorism seems to take another direction. Schmid divides conceptually the notions of "mala-per se" (evil in itself) from mala prohibita (prohibited by the statute or the law). While the latter encompasses acts which are legally punishable because they remain, outlaw, the former appeals to grave offences which by nature should be punished no matter the culture or the state (Schmid 2004). The terrorist crimes fall in the mala-per-se definition but no less true is that terrorism takes the room in the constellations of the political conflict. This means that previous political tensions or the lack of a robust legal framework to create political stability may be two key factors for the rise of terrorism. As Schmid goes no to write,

"Due to globalisation, the permeability of borders and state interdependence, the internationalisation of terrorism and other forms of political violence is a fact. Terrorism needs to be studied in the broader contexts of political conflict, taking into account both governing state and opposition parties and their allies in society" (Schmid, 2004: 201)

In view of this scenario, wars are fought within the limits or the legal borders of the international code. This does not apply to terrorist acts. Although he is self-esteemed as a warrior, the terrorist defies not only the codes of the war but also the principle of non-combatant security. Those who are not in the hub of operations should not be hurt. As non-state actors, in some case, terrorists often use indiscriminate violence to impose a message to "Others".

"While a political assassination juxtaposes the murderer (or the one who has been ordered to do it) with the victim, the terrorist act is based on an indirect strategy: a randomly chosen or representative victim is killed in public but the ultimate addressees of the victimisation are one or several target audiences: others from the group of the victim, the public at large, or, more narrowly, members of the constituency of the terrorist. In other words, terrorist violence is mainly perpetrated for its effects on others rather than the immediate victims (who might be dead)" (Ibid: 207).

As cited above, terrorists are oriented to cause intimidation through the violence exerted against a third person, the victim. Once done, the media does the rest. The attack is covered creating serious problems for the local governance. Schmid (2004)

holds the thesis an act of terrorism should be framed as a criminal and at the same time a political act which needs from a semiotic discourse to prosper. For this reason, it is important to study the psychological dimension of terrorist violence in society. In this token, in a prefatory introduction to his book Terrorism: the philosophical issues, claims that terrorism cannot be morally justified questioning its troubled or complex nature. Some scholars believe mistakenly that terrorists are primarily victims who have been educated in violent and unstable homes. At best, there are some grounds that justify terrorism arguing it is the fight of weaker against the stronger. Terrorists violate the basic human rights victimizing innocent citizens to achieve their political ends. As he bemoans,

"Acts of terrorism they committed would be violations of human rights of the victims and thus clearly and gravely unjust; but the need to prevent the unspeakable the imminent and human disaster in store for it might be thought to carry even greater weight, and therefore to provide moral justification for those acts" (Primoratz, 2004: xviii)

At a closer look, Primoratz lays the ethical foundations to forge a new debate revolving around the effects of terrorism but he does not show any effort to resolve the philosophical dilemmas of multiculturalism. To put this in bluntly, what laws should be applied when the hosting nation does not conduct a thorough investigation about terrorist attacks or support financially the involving terrorist cells?

A preliminary answer to this question aims to the following axiom: those nations which promote terrorism should be militarily intervened to be re-framed within the borders of the democracy. An affirmation of this nature not only is ethnocentric – assuming that western democratic nations do not support terrorist- but also it ignores the limitations of the Kantian peace to be pragmatically applied in international affairs. This exhibits a simplification of a much deep-seated issue. What is equally important, dividing the world into secure or unsecure nations seems not to be an accurate diagnosis of the problem.

The dynamics of event management is pretty different than other tourist destinations. The security in events remains closed or strictly circumscribed to a specific venue while in normal conditions the destination is open to unknown visitors. The security forces are aware of the steps to follow and the check-up controls in the organization of events. In fact, events are organized within a timeframe while a classic destination is operating in the year. So, terrorists can take in favour of the surprise factor. This explains why in event management the probabilities of terrorist attacks are notably fewer than in classic destinations. One of the aspects that potentiates the fear in the city seems to be related to the fact that anyone can be a victim of terrorism, anytime and anywhere. In the organization of events, this goes in a contrasting dimension. They are limited to a specific geographical point which can be closely scrutinized. Legally speaking, the laws of the hosting country are used at the time of judging the terrorists though some super-powers –when their compatriots have been harmed- ask for a process of extradition. Secondly, as professor Howie (2018) highlights, some security guards are low-paid or subject to excessive working hours. This precaritizes not only their labour conditions but cements the possibilities they were seduced to liberate the zone or having a complicit gaze of the attacks. Howie adds that the capitalist system rests on the contradictory basis because it valorises security as one of the mainstream values while at the bottom undermines the role of security guards and other workers. Last but not least, the lack of legal cooperation among the countries makes very hard an international alliance to prevent terrorist attacks. The frustrated attacks in Rio reveal that the local community plays a leading role in advising the security forces of potential attacks. The Muslim community in Rio de Janeiro alerted the authorities on the presence of unknown Syrian agents who conspired in the darkness to commit an attack. Unlike Europe, this happens simply because the Arab community in Latin America, -i.e. in countries as Argentina or Brazil- is historically integrated into the culture. These dimensions –international, national and cultural- are of importance in the organization of festivals and events. What is clear, is the lack of shared international laws that prevent the radical violence of terrorist groups. This begs a more than thorny question, is event management the precondition to over-tourism?, is over-tourism the sign of the hostility against the Stranger or simply the aftermaths of a pour planning and communication?

Challenges of Tourism and Event Management.

At a first glimpse, the relation of over-tourism and the hostility are inextricably intertwined. Nonetheless, the interconnection between terrorism and over-tourism seems not to be so clear. Over the years, scholars strongly believed that tourism was a growing industry which will bring prosperity, political stability and democracy to the non-western nations. Based on the belief that the tourism industry was a direct consequence from the democratic maturation of developed economies, these voices alerted on the problem of psychological resentment sometimes nourished in the hosting communities when the local forms of subsistence are not taken for granted. The host-guest encounters are given on a deep material asymmetry which paves the ways for the rise of hostile reactions against foreign tourists. However, in the recent decades, above all just after 9/11, a new radical wave emerged to debate to what extent the tourism industry is really affected by terrorism (Bianchi 2006; Bianchi & Stephenson, 2013; Korstanje & Clayton 2012).

In this respect, Korstanje & Clayton (2012) interrogate to what extent tourism and terrorism are two complementing forces orchestrated to domesticate the lay-citizen. In other words, while anarchists –in the former centuries- struggled and conducted terrorist attacks in order for their claims gain further visibility, other subtle group known as "anarcho-syndicalist" worked hard together the unions to impose substantial labour reforms such as less working hours and better salaries which paradoxically facilitated the first organized travels. Citing Foucault, Korstanje & Clayton acknowledge that any risk should be defined as a domesticated threat. The society deploys its disciplinary mechanism to locate, domesticate and incorporate those external dangers that can place it in jeopardy. Through the imposition of leisure-travels, the ruling elite successfully domesticated the violence of the pioneering anarchists. Like a vaccine, which in medical terms is an inoculated virus, terrorism (as well as anarchist) is tourism by other means. What is equally important, for these researchers, the tourism industry not only would not be directly affected by international terrorism but also it evenly recovers the tourist fluxes once the time elapses. Sites like the Ground-zero receives more visitors today in the dark days of 9/11. This occurs because the violence against tourists wakes up the dormant sentiment of reciprocity which enhances the social cohesion (Sather-Wagstaff 2016). With this background in mind, one might speculate that over-tourism is the end an epoch, the end of an age, or tourism –at least- as we know it (Hannam 2009). Not surprisingly some the banners or graffiti against mass tourism says "Tourist: you are the real terrorists!", "Tourists kill the city", "Tourists are bastards" or "Tourists go home!". Here two main reflections should be done. On one hand, in the society of scale production, the tourists were seen as a "friend" who someday can come back! a stranger who should be welcomed because of the mulplicator effects. The 9/11, followed by the stock market crisis in 2008, was a turning point whether the "non-western Other" became in a "non-desired Other". The higher levels of anxiety and uncertainty generated by terrorism, where the neighbours may be suspected to collaborate with radical cells, can be only curbed through the hostility against the alterity. Anthropologically speaking, human beings relate with the known alterity in three levels: sympathy, hostility or indifference. While the "distant-Other" is venerated or feared –ie the case of God or the Demon), the "close-Other" is subdued and domesticated. In the days of globalization, where the earth is flat, -for some people literally- the old borders between the selfhood and the alterity have been blurred. The distant Other who lives in the urban cities –pressed by the colonial exploitation and the humanitarian urgency of migration is being prosecuted and jailed as suspected of terrorism, while the "close-Other" (the tourist who shares the western values) should be protected. The terrorists are natives who certainly hate the society where they live, while tourists are a real stranger converted in a citizen (a knight) of the global order. While the leisure travels in the past centuries had the imperialist imprint, which suggests that travels are cultural forms of colonization and education, today travels traverse a multicultural landscape where the Ethnic-difference coalesces in the uniqueness. This point was ideologically mutating towards the opposite landscape: today, modern tourists are seen as terrorists!. On another, the relation of the process of touristification, which means the expansion and mass exploitation of the site by the greed of local and international tour operators appears no to be very easy to grasp. Even in Argentina, India or Brazil, many highly-demanded sites do not experience the rise of anti-tourist movements.

CONCLUSION

Over recent years, the public spectacle and media events become a fertile ground for terrorist attacks. Particularly, media events play a leading role in enhancing the social cohesion as well as revitalizing the psychological frustrations happened during the working days. Paradoxically, terrorism needs from maximizing their gains while the costs are minimized. As Sandler and Enders put it, the spectacularisation tourism and events offer is a double-edged sword. The same attractiveness that makes of our global cities a safer place to live is employed by the terrorist cells to cause chaos and uncertainty. The present chapter discussed theoretically the difficult interrelation between terrorism and event management as well as the conceptual limitations of western rationality to understand the "undesired Other". While the security in event management is easier to organize than in a city because of the surprise factor, no less true is that terrorism operates globally in the dimensions of an absence of shared legislation that can be internationally applied.

REFERENCES

Altheide, D. (2017). *Terrorism and the Politics of fear*. New York: Rowman & Littlefield.

Altheide, D. L. (2004). Consuming terrorism. *Symbolic Interaction*, *27*(3), 289–308. doi:10.1525i.2004.27.3.289

Arana, J. E., & León, C. J. (2008). The impact of terrorism on tourism demand. *Annals of Tourism Research*, *35*(2), 299–315. doi:10.1016/j.annals.2007.08.003

Bianchi, R. (2006). Tourism and the globalisation of fear: Analysing the politics of risk and (in) security in global travel. *Tourism and Hospitality Research*, *7*(1), 64–74. doi:10.1057/palgrave.thr.6050028

Bianchi, R. V., & Stephenson, M. L. (2013). Deciphering tourism and citizenship in a globalized world. *Tourism Management*, *39*, 10–20. doi:10.1016/j.tourman.2013.03.006

Chomsky, N. (2015). *Culture of terrorism*. London: Haymarket Books.

Coleman, M. (2003). The naming of 'terrorism'and evil 'outlaws': Geopolitical place-making after 11 September. *Geopolitics*, *8*(3), 87–104. doi:10.1080/14650040412331307722

Dayan, D., & Katz, E. (1994). *Media events*. Cambridge: Harvard University Press.

Eid, M. (Ed.). (2014). *Exchanging terrorism oxygen for media airwaves: The age of terroredia: The age of terroredia*. Hershey: IGI Global. doi:10.4018/978-1-4666-5776-2

Enders, W., & Sandler, T. (2011). *The political economy of terrorism*. Cambridge: Cambridge University Press. doi:10.1017/CBO9780511791451

Epifanio, M. (2011). Legislative response to international terrorism. *Journal of Peace Research*, *48*(3), 399–411. doi:10.1177/0022343311399130

Hall, C. M., Timothy, D. J., & Duval, D. T. (2004). Security and tourism: Towards a new understanding? *Journal of Travel & Tourism Marketing*, *15*(2-3), 1–18. doi:10.1300/J073v15n02_01

Hannam, K. (2009). The end of tourism? Nomadology and the mobilities paradigm. Philosophical Issues in Tourism, 37, 101.

Hoskins, A., & O' Loughlin, B. (2007). *Television and terror: Conflicting times and the crisis of news discourse*. New York: Springer. doi:10.1057/9780230592810

Howie, L. (2012). Witnessing terrorism. In *Witnesses to Terror* (pp. 155–175). Basingstoke: Palgrave Macmillan. doi:10.1057/9781137271761_8

Huntington, S. (2002). *The Clash of Civilization: and the remaking of the World Order*. New York: Simon Schuster.

Keohane, D. (2005). *The EU and counter-terrorism*. London: Centre for European Reform.

Keohane, N. O., & Zeckhauser, R. J. (2003). The ecology of terror defense. In *The Risks of Terrorism* (pp. 103–131). Boston, MA: Springer. doi:10.1007/978-1-4757-6787-2_6

Kepel, G. (2017). *Terror in France: The rise of jihad in the west* (Vol. 64). Princeton: Princeton University Press.

Korstanje, M. E., & Clayton, A. (2012). Tourism and terrorism: Conflicts and commonalities. *Worldwide Hospitality and Tourism Themes*, *4*(1), 8–25. doi:10.1108/17554211211198552

Mawby, R. I. (2000). Tourists' Perceptions of Security: The Risk—Fear Paradox. *Tourism Economics*, *6*(2), 109–121. doi:10.5367/000000000101297514

McCauley, C., & Moskalenko, S. (2014). Some Things We Think We've Learned Since 9/11: A Commentary on Marc Sageman's "The Stagnation in Terrorism Research". *Terrorism and Political Violence*, *26*(4), 601–606. doi:10.1080/09546553.2014.895653

Pipes, D. (1986). The scourge of suicide terrorism. *National Interest*, (4): 95–99.

Primoratz, I. (2004). Introduction. In I. Primoratz (Ed.), *Terrorism: the philosophical issues* (pp. x–xxiv). New York: Palgrave-Macmillan. doi:10.1057/9780230204546

Quarantelli, E. L. (Ed.). (2005). *What is a disaster? A dozen perspectives on the question*. Abingdon: Routledge. doi:10.4324/9780203984833

Richter, L. K., & Waugh, W. L. Jr. (1986). Terrorism and tourism as logical companions. *Tourism Management*, *7*(4), 230–238. doi:10.1016/0261-5177(86)90033-6

Ryan, C. (1993). Crime, violence, terrorism and tourism: An accidental or intrinsic relationship? *Tourism Management*, *14*(3), 173–183. doi:10.1016/0261-5177(93)90018-G

Sageman, M. (2014). The stagnation in terrorism research. *Terrorism and Political Violence*, *26*(4), 565–580. doi:10.1080/09546553.2014.895649

Sather-Wagstaff, J. (2016). *Heritage that hurts: Tourists in the memoryscapes of September 11*. Abingdon: Routledge. doi:10.4324/9781315427539

Schmid, A. P. (2004). Frameworks for conceptualising terrorism. *Terrorism and Political Violence*, *16*(2), 197–221. doi:10.1080/09546550490483134

Skoll, G. (2010). *Social theory of fear: Terror, torture, and death in a post-capitalist world*. New York: Springer.

Sönmez, S. F. (1998). Tourism, terrorism, and political instability. *Annals of Tourism Research*, *25*(2), 416–456. doi:10.1016/S0160-7383(97)00093-5

Spivey, N. (2005). *The Ancient Olympics*. Oxford: Oxford University Press.

Stampnitzky, L. (2013). *Disciplining terror: How experts invented 'terrorism*. Cambridge: Cambridge University Press. doi:10.1017/CBO9781139208161

Sylas, E. I. (2006). *Terrorism: A Global Scourge*. New York: Author-House.

Tarlow, P. (2014). *Tourism security: strategies for effectively managing travel risk and safety*. Oxford: Elsevier.

Tarlow, P. (2017). *Sport Travel Security*. Oxford: Elsevier.

Taylor, T., & Toohey, K. (2005). Impacts of terrorism-related safety and security measures at a major sport event. *Event Management*, *9*(4), 199–209. doi:10.3727/152599506776771544

Toohey, K., & Taylor, T. (2008). Mega events, fear, and risk: Terrorism at the Olympic Games. *Journal of Sport Management*, *22*(4), 451–469. doi:10.1123/jsm.22.4.451

Chapter 7 Health and Safety in Events Management

Ian Arnott
University of Sunderland, London, UK

ABSTRACT

Health and safety in events management is essential and needs to be undertaken and understood both at a practitioner level as well as academically. The subject area has created a lot of interest due to the various case studies of events that have received attention due to, in some cases, poor practices leading to substantial media and public awareness. Therefore, its management needs to be seen as a priority and an area that needs to be understood greatly. The aim of health and safety management is to ensure that all the participants and attendees, as well as those affected by an event, are protected from threats to their health and safety.

INTRODUCTION

Health and safety in events management is essential and needs to be undertaken and understood both at a practitioner level as well as academically. The subject area has been created a lot of interest due to the various case studies of events that have received attention due to, in some cases, poor practices leading to substantial media and public awareness. Therefore, its management needs to be seen as a priority and an area that needs to be understood greatly.

The aim of Health and safety management is to ensure that all the participants and attendees, as well as those affected by an event, are protected from threats to their health and safety (Gertz, 2012). What also be noted, in particular in the events industry which can be very diverse in its nature from localised events such as a

DOI: 10.4018/978-1-7998-3230-0.ch007

country fete be held in an afternoon to staging an Olympic event that can be spread over 14 + days that it is very fast and ever changing. This leads to the perceptions that health and safety can change due to the size and magnitude of an event. Also in the past, there has been a tendency to view health and safety issues as 'red tape; bureaucracy that merely tricks regulatory boxes whilst creating extra work for event practitioners (Bladen, Kennell, Abson and Wilde, 2012). However due to the stringent processes that now regulate the delivery of events of all shapes and sizes the safe implementation of health and safety policies need to be implemented no matter at what level. People who attend, which has already mentioned earlier, is the highest priority for any event team. The risks in this part of the event management's responsibilities are enormous – both to the event and all the key stakeholders (Bowdin, Allen, OToole, Harris and Mcdonnell, 2011). Prevention and mitigation are the first line of defence, which must be followed by proper monitoring and timely response to procedures. Safety hazards are usually easy to see and typically have immediate consequences (Rutherford Silvas, 2013). Health hazards, however are often harder to recognise because the effects of exposure may have delayed consequences (Rossol, 2000). So the results of an incident from not conducting or identifying the appropriate potential health and safety issues can potential have a long term impact of any other events of a similar nature and potential the impact to the wider industry (Bowdin et al, 2011). In the United Kingdom there have been similar examples where health and safety practices have been implicated in such areas as football where at Hillsborough Football disaster which lead to the change in football stadia design and seating where countless fans were 96 crushed to their death and 766 people reported with injuries (The Telegraph, 2009). This clearly led to a marked change in the football stadia was designed thereafter when it became compulsory that all grounds had to spectator seating and fencing was removed so that should situations arise that the access to open areas could be gained avoiding such incidents happening again where mass gathering of individuals are taking place.

Mass gatherings are an increasingly a common feature in events management and they are often bring together organisations that do not normally interact, and the large number of attendees and stakeholders involved represents an enormous amount of planning and a logistic challenge (Bistatrki, Mckeown & Kyratsis, 2019). Such events usually represent significant challenges that can affect health and safety sectors of host towns, regions and countries (Flabouris, Nocera, & Garner, 2004; Meehan, Tomney, Drinnon, Cunningham, Anderson & Baker, 1998). The distinctive features of these events that can affect health and safety planning and the services that maybe need to be involved or even called upon could encompass a large geographical spread, large levels of attendance, event duration as well as the potential security concerns (Delorenzo, 1997). So what is clearly evident from this that no matter what size that health and safety legislation needs to be at the forefront of all planning matters to avert or eliminate the possibilities of any type of incident potentially taking place? Without proper attention to health, safety and risk management, event organisers expose their audience, their colleagues and their contractors to injury or worst case scenario loss of life (Bladen, . et.al 2012).

What has to be acknowledged that a clearer understanding and exploration of the true meaning of health and safety and the frameworks has to be presented for the potential implementation for event organisers? What can be understood that ramifications can impact of not only the event but the industry as a whole in the short and long term? The importance is further understood and by the model put forward by Bladen et al, (2012) in figure 1.

Figure 1. The Importance of Health and Safety (Adapted from Bladen et al, 2012)

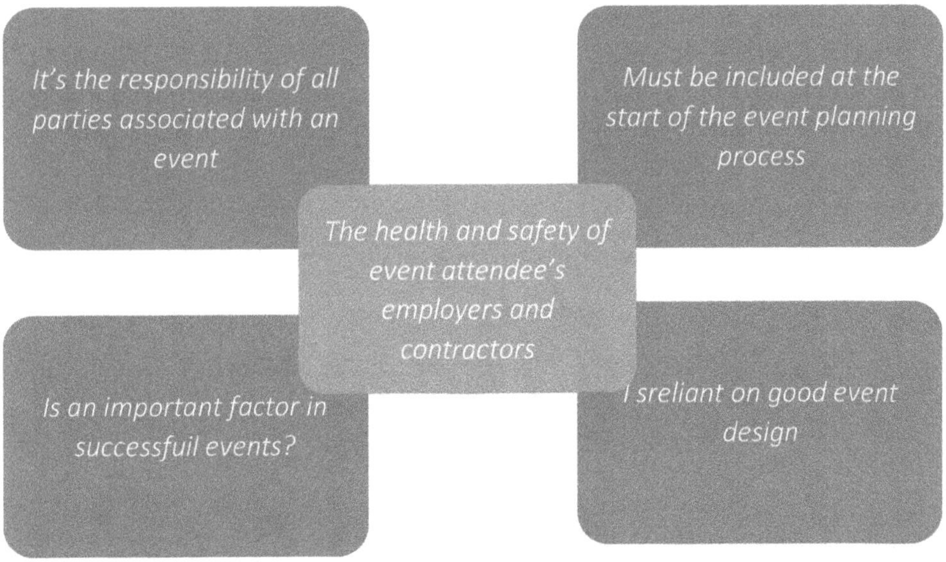

Health and Safety Frameworks and Management systems in Events

Health and Safety management systems and frameworks are an essential part in methodical planning for events management as they provide a useful starting point for any practitioner who is undertaking event design. In doing so it allows the event organiser to consider a range of significant aspects of event planning –venue and site design-to circumstantial issues, such as refreshments and sanitation (Health and Safety Executive, 2015).

So therefore, Health and Safety by adopting such management systems and frameworks aims to:

"Ensure all participants and attendees, as well as those affected by an event, are protected to their health and safety. It is people-focused, and includes the very important crowd management and security tasks" (Getz and Page, 2016)

Getz and Page (2016) in table 1outlines some of the key areas that in planning and developing a framework or management systems for event practitioners to see where is cross overs with others.

So what can be clearly noted from Getz and Page (2016) that from Risk, Health and Safety through to the unique event issues and applications health and safety systems and frameworks help to develop good practices through a structured and systematic management approach (Chang and Liang, 2009).

In order to have a successful system/ framework it is essential to understand all the steps that need to be taken into consideration and they have to be developed very clearly the event project management and are pre-during and post event as is highlighted in

Figure 2. Risk, Health and Safety (Adapted from Getz and Page, 2016)

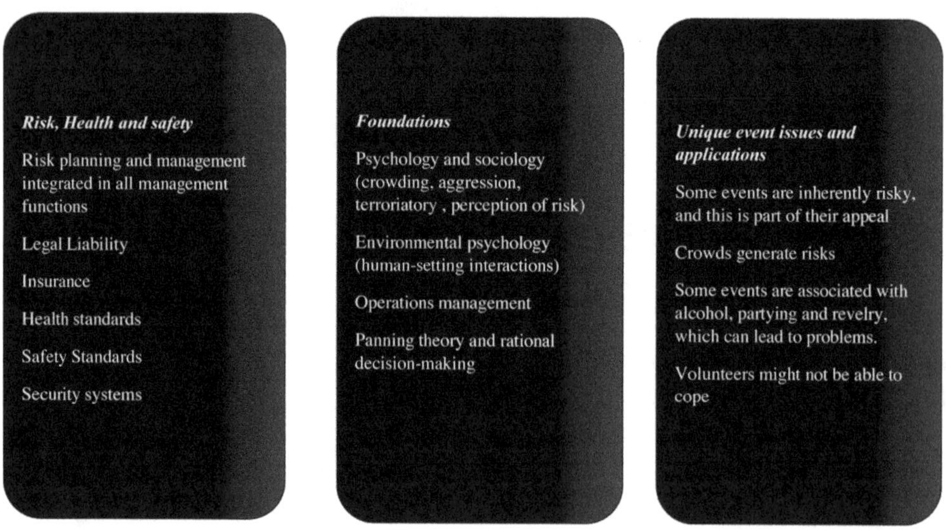

Table 1 takes into consideration some of the areas that need to be thought about when developing systems and frameworks for an event. However, every event is

unique and table 1 provides a small snapshot of some of the areas that will need to be thought about/ planned for and serves as useful guidance.

Table 1. Event Management Health and Safety Considerations

Pre-event (Project management considerations)	During	Post event
Venue/ facility Event Design Accessibility suppliers/ contractors Parking and crowd management considerations Crowd/ spectator/ participant movement Stewards/ support staff H & S training Event timetable/ Order of events Delivery of Equipment/ Infrastructure Event Communications Safety staff specialists	Crowd/ spectator/ participant movement Stewards/ support staff First Aid staff Safety staff specialists Transport/ logistics/ supplies Fire Safety Specific incident related management Contingency due to adverse weather or specific areas related to the event	Crowd/ spectator/ participant dispersal Car parking exiting management Removal/ dismantling of event infrastructure

Kim, Abdul Rahim, Iranmesh and Forogughi (2019) present a conceptual model/ framework (Figure 3l) for event management involving the key stakeholders who could assist in the development of an event management framework.

Figure 3. Conceptual Model for Event Management (Adapted from Kim.et.al, 2019)

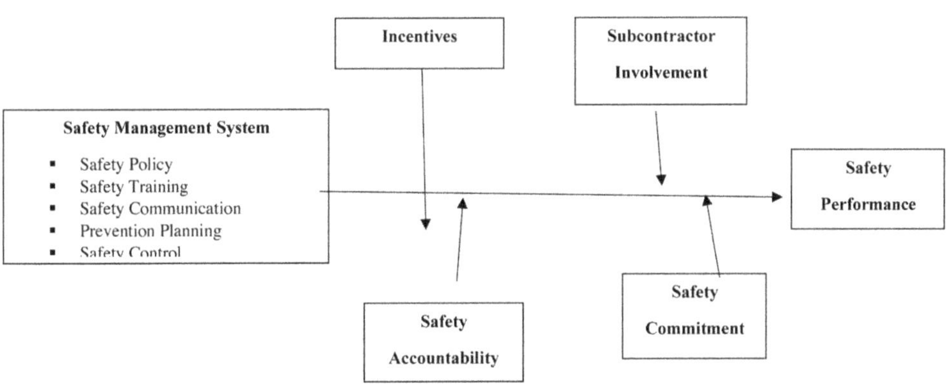

The model is useful as it serves as guidance for the event manager and its primary objective is to develop good practice in the industry and also generally across other areas. Ghahramani and Salmien (2019) support this ideology however, like all systems they stress that the appropriate implementation of the adopted area. To prevent accidents and ensure good event safety event managers have made great efforts to find factors that may affect successful implementation of safety management systems. Various factors have been identified, such as accident analysis, risk assessment, emergency response, communication and report (Demichela and Piccini, 2006; Teo and Ling, 2006; Kelly and Berger, 2006, Basso et al., 2004).

The most important in all of the planning when all the key factors are being considered of potential accidents is that event managers is that they consider the Health and Safety at Work (HSW) Act 1974. This is the primary piece of legalisation of people that work within the United Kingdom (UK) and is an example of national legislation that affects the events industry.

The HSW sets out the general principles of managing health and safety at work, and enables the creation of requirements through such regulations as the Control of Substances Hazardous to Health Regulations 2002 (COSHH) and the Management of Health and Safety at Work Regulations 1999 (MHSW).

In the delivery of events in the UK the HSW is the most important guidance and legislation to which the events industry must adhere to no matter what size it is (Bladen et al, 2012). It makes mandatory for all employees to conduct risk assessment of their work activity which can be implemented and written into a system similar to that one presented by Kim.et.al (2019). It also allows a systematic framework for event managers to follow and implement it effectively hopefully ensuring that any type of eventuality might be considered and written into a risk assessment.

With the heightened awareness of terrorism following the September 11, 2001 terrorist's attacks has caused many travellers to make their destination choices using security criterion (Ferdniand & Kitchin, 2017; Hall et al., 2003; Sonmez and Graefe, 1998). This was further confirmed by study conducted by Kim and Chalip (2004) on the 2002 FIFA World Cup, where it as found that attendance at the World Cup was affected by respondents concerns over safety risks. Sporting events are often potential targets of terrorist's threats due to the events scale and the amount of media attention (Cielslak, 2009; Taylor and Toohey, 2006). The results demonstrate the importance of sustaining the event with effective safety and security practices (Ferdinand and Kitchin, 2017) and those that are shaped and modelled through good and effective frameworks.

Even events that are not as big as World Cup or Olympics that might be held over a longer period of time with mass both attendance and participation need to have robust frameworks and systems in place. Other big events that can be seen a special with a mass attendance on one day can be a Marathon such as London where 26,000 people are running through the streets of London to those with an attendance 15,000. Those they are a one off they do take place annual and are highly complex from a health, safety and security perspective. Furthermore there special events that may only take place such as the Queen in England's Birthday with a huge security sweep and security management with dignitaries as well as a mass attendance of people descending on the nation's capital in London. All of those celebrating a special event and potentially could be a one off require a deep and highly complex logistical management within their nature. What it is clearly noted no matter what size or magnitude careful consideration needs to go into their planning. Smaller events, though these may not have as many logistical areas that may need considering they can still by very complex within their nature from a one of celebration of a local villages centenary of even a wedding. They maybe of a simplistic nature but these events are very special within their own right and need to be well thought out.

Health and Safety in Special Events

Special events have to been discussed briefly previously but what exactly is a special event? The term 'special events' has been coined to describe specific rituals, presentations, performances or celebrations that are consciously planned and created to mark special occasions and/ or to achieve particular social, cultural or corporate goals and objectives (Bowdin et al, 2008). Getz (2005) puts forward a further two definitions shared by event practitioners who are delivering and also one from an event consumer:

§ *A special event is a one-time or infrequently occurring event outside normal programmes or activities of the sponsoring or organising body*

§ *To the customer or guest, a special event is an opportunity for a leisure, social or cultural experience outside the normal range of choices or beyond everyday experience*

Whatever the definitions the most important thing to consider the attributes Getz (2005) believes they create a sense of 'specialness' are festive spirit, uniqueness, quality, authenticity, tradition, hospitality, theme and symbolism. This could be such celebrations as welcoming in the New Year where the event organiser is dealing with pyrotechnics and ensuring that all elements of health and safety are taking into consideration as well as the crowd management. Therefore the conceptual model (figure 3) put forward by Kim et al (2019) would be an essential model/ system due to the number of stakeholders that would be involved. As well as the number of stakeholders, especially events that could be a one off celebration may need a variety of emergency services involved as well as the local authority and many more groups. In such cases this might be in the form of Event Advisory Groups (EAG) Safety Advisory Groups (SAG) who have a variety of people who may have to be involved with the event or have a vested interest in the event taking place. Their role would be clearly in the capacity of offering guidance and support to event practitioners or an event agency intending to deliver an event.

Such event/ safety advisory groups may be structured like that one presented in figure 4 where a number of external agencies are like this one in South Lakes in Cumbria in the United Kingdom where event organisers have to complete paperwork and provide various documentation (Appendix A, B, C) to support their applications to put on an event.

Figure 4. Event Advisory Group Structure (South Lakes, Cumbria United Kingdom)

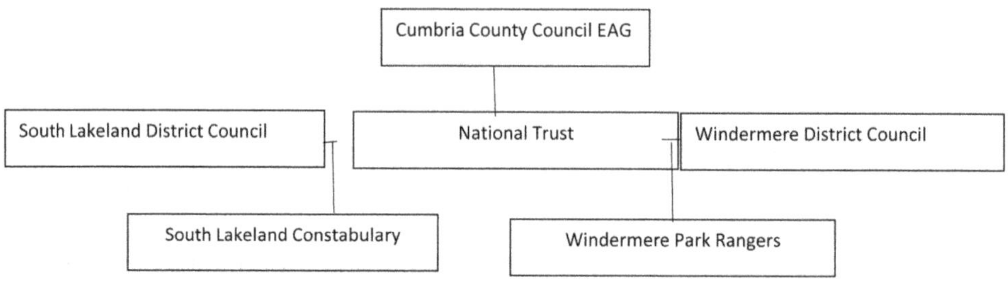

The nature and size of a special event has been highlighted with some examples therefore it can vary and the event organiser should treat this the same as any other event no matter if it is only for one day. Many people during the Queen's Diamond (Case Study 1) Jubilee celebration to the streets to have street parties. However, the organisation involved a variety key areas therefore for this one off celebration guidance was being offered on how to do this as case study one highlights.

Case Study 1

Queens Diamond Jubilee: How to Organise a Party

Hundreds of people across the country have already written to their local councils to express their desire to hold public celebrations on the weekend of the Queen's Diamond Jubilee weekend..

Early figures suggest more street parties will be thrown to celebrate the Queen's Diamond Jubilee this year than were held for the royal wedding.

Organisers predict the summer weather and the example set by last spring's festivities could see up to three million people take to the streets in June 2012.

There are a few different kinds of street parties that can be held. Here's a guide to help you get started.

1. All local council websites carry information and instructions about how to organise a basic “small street party”. Councils have asked to be told about the event four to 12 weeks ahead of time. Be prepared to answer questions or fill out an application form.

The application form will ask for details about when and what time the party will take place. You will also be asked to give information about road traffic and closures and whether any properties or businesses will be affected. The council will then get back to you.

The community group Streets Alive offer advice such as having a neighbours’ picnic in a local park or moving a couple of cars and slinging up bunting on a pavement.

2. If the street party is going to take up more space and you want to close a road, the local council must give permission. Bus routes and whether emergency services have access will be considered. Also road closure signs will be necessary. Hire them from the local council or make them yourself using Streets Alive’s instructions, cardboard and a colour printer.
3. The third type of part is a “street meet”. This is celebration without closing a road, held in a park, drive or cul-de-sac. Streets Alive holds a lot of useful information about how to organise this kind of get together.
4. The fourth and final option it to hold a Big Lunch on Sunday June 3. This is an Eden Project initiative that started in 2009. It aims to get as many people as possible across the whole of the UK to have lunch with their neighbours in a simple act of community, friendship and fun. This year, it coincides with the Queen’s Diamond Jubilee

The Queen has given it her official stamp of approval and celebrities such as Boris Johnson, Hugh Fearnley-Whittingstall and Carol Smillie are also in support.

The benefit of going through this route is that the Big Lunch team will help you plan, answer questions and provide a pack full of hints, tips and ideas.

Downing Street is encouraging residents to challenge councils that attempt to charge for road closures or that insist on public liability insurance for the Jubilee celebrations.

Various councils have already started planning for June’s festivities. Basildon Council is planning a free party in a box scheme, including party hats, flags, balloons, bunting, posters, a disposable camera and suggestions for games on the day.

East Dorset Council has set up a £30,000 grant fund to help groups celebrating either the Diamond Jubilee or the Olympics, Newark and Sherwood District Council has a similar £20,000 fund for events over the Jubilee weekend.

Basingstoke and Deane Borough Council is arranging blanket insurance to cover activities at most events on public land such as street parties, while Kent County Council is waiving charges for street parties on quiet residential roads.

Find out what your council is planning via their website.

People will hold their street parties on either the Saturday or the Sunday of the Jubilee weekend.

The Jubilee River Pageant, the central event of the weekend, will take place on the Saturday. This will feature a seven-mile long flotilla of 1,000 boats from around the world processing down the Thames led by the Queen in the Royal Barge.

As the Queens Diamond Jubilee case study highlights suggests such areas as road closures maybe required and also work with councils to ensure a great number of elements are addressed and are covered. This also may work with the local council's events officer offering guidance on Health and Safety plans for those organising committees who may not have considered the elements before. Also what must be noted from this that even this type of an event is temporary in its nature all the eventualities need to be considered in the planning and design stages (pre-event). What is also clear that such events brings communities together in cohesion and are typically more localised, especially when they are, in this case, street based but also bigger Mega Events with thousands of people descending on central London to be part of the event taking place.

Health and Safety in Local / Community Events.

In the previous section Localised/ community events have been discussed and some of the guidelines and issues that have to be considered in these and the types of people who would attend these. What is useful to know about these types of events, as well as in some cases which has been highlighted celebrations, they are can primarily for social and the entertainment value (Bowdin et al, 2011).

It is worth noting that various definitions have been put forward such as Janiskee (1996):

Family-fun events that are considered 'owned' by a community because they use volunteer services from the host community, employ public venues such as streets, parks and schools and are produced at the direction of local government agencies or non-government organisations (NGO\s) such as service clubs, public safety organisations or business associations.

What is interesting with regards to the definition that has been put forward is closing examples that these types of events are focused on and Janiskee (1996) shares that 'public safety organisations'. These can vary from the fire services and those types of providers through to the Ambulance service etc. Needless to say when considering Health and Safety in events management these types of organisations will be part of event safety advisory groups who will be able to best serve and support Local/ Community events and event's organisers. Further examples of events of this nature could be a school fair, a church fete and various other charitable events.

Even with, what could be considered simplistic events as charitable events these still have the movement of people, electrics, PA systems, fire hazards, potential temporary structures, car parking potentially and many other areas' clearly will need to have key considerations when it comes to Health and Safety planning.

Though the complexities of these types of events can last a few hours, ½ or even a full day the volume of people tend to be more contained to the numbers that actually come and therefore can be easier to manage not those of a major event who attract a significant number of people.

Health and Safety in Major Events

Health and Safety in Major Events can vary due to the nature of the type of within itself due to the nature of them as they could vary from being at one specific venue such International Amateur Athletic Federation Diamond League meet taking place in an athletic stadia where people are contained within one environment. Whereas this can be variable where there maybe multi sites for warming up etc. such as Henley Regata and people lined up along the shores of the river Thames. Needless to say this offering another dimension for consideration when it comes to Health Safety Management and planning.

Whatever the event being if whether the event was at one venue or multiple ones all health and safety management systems need to mirror each other so that the frameworks/ models and the policies can work effectively.

Though the discussion is clearly about health and safety what is a major event in the context of this field? One definition put forward about major events is that from Van der Wagen and White (2018):

Major events attract significant local interest and a large number of participants as well as generat8ing significant tourism revenue.

Though Van der wagen and White's (2018) view is relevant but it is very broad and from applying a clear understanding for health and safety management as far back as two decades UK Sport (1999a) provides some clearer direction put forward that it contains three elements:

It must involve competition between teams and / or individuals representing a number of nations.

It must attract significant public interest nationally and internationally, through spectator attendance and media coverage.

It must be of international significance to the sport concerned and feature prominently on its international calendar.

Though UK Sports (1999a) view focuses on specifically sport each element can be applied to a music concert where it could be annually where top artists/ musicians playing on stage in a city annually.

Such events would heavily involve a great number of stakeholders, specifically in safety/ event advisory groups. The complexity and detail would have to be intricate in the planning element and health and safety would, due to magnitude and size, of the event would have a key working group alone. This group would work with such organisations as the police, road traffic management companies, fire service, ambulance service, stewarding companies and other external agencies in the delivery of the event itself and their health, safety and risk management requirements. Therefore Kim et al's (2019) conceptual model (figure 3) would be very relevant and apply in this case. Also there would be a heavy liaison with all the key stakeholder in the SAG/EAG and this would monthly ensuring that all the key stages are implemented for all aspects of the event.

As well as health and safety management for the event there would be occupational health and safety management systems (OHSMS) due to the number of people that would either be volunteers or paid employees leading up to, during or post the event.

Occupational health and safety (OHS) is essential for the wellbeing of workers from the stand point of practices and policies to be adopted by event companies (Couto da Silva, Amaral, 2019) the emphasis, particularly within events management, is the importance of providing a healthy environment and it considers the basic individuals characteristics and social relations, control of incidents and accidents (Ackapovi and Dizmaikumah, 2016; Rajaprasd and Chalapthi, 2015)

OHSMS are either mandatory or voluntary according (Robson et al, 2007). However due to the potential complexities of event management and nature of the roles that are undertaken, e.g. an individual or teams may undertake a variety roles. Therefore when it comes to event management the event organisation has the responsibility for the safety of all its employees. In the UK, this is covered by the Corporate Manslaughter Handbook Act (2007) (Bladen et al, 2012). These laws sate that adequate safety practices and procedures must be in place, and they allow for conviction if it can be proved beyond reasonable doubt that an events organisation in this case, was homicidally reckless about risk (Bladen et al, 2012; Slapper, 2007). Needless to say when it comes to events no matter what size they are, this applies to accidental death of both employees and attendees. However this can only be applied if the events company is at fault and not by an external situation caused by terrorism for example. This has been in such situations like the Boston Marathon where multiple explosions took place near the finish during the event. Though this highlights that the event organiser was not at fault it serves as an example that from a security perspective that sports event organisers in particular where there hundreds of spectators lining the routes this needs to be built into their health, safety and risk management systems and models. In such instances for those types of events that are very similar to a major event are Hallmark events which can be linked to Carnivals.

Health and Safety and Hallmark Events

There have been very many views shared about what hallmark events are, so therefore placing health and safety could be tricky? Though this is so Ritchie (1984) defines them as:

Major one time or recurring events of limited duration, developed primarily to enhance awareness, appeal and profitability of tourism destination in the short or long term. Such events rely for their success in uniqueness, status or timely significance to create interest and attract attention.

Examples of these types of events like could be some sporting events where they are trying to give some sort of economic impact for the hosting city bringing not only athletes but their families and extended ones also. There are also annual music festivals such as one in the North of East England called the mouth of the Tyne festival which celebrates its heritage.

The implications for health and safety for this type or not to dissimilar than that of a major event as they both carry very similar characteristics and can be put under the same umbrella as they are both major and their attendance both by those working at the events and also those who are participating/ attending it also.

The engagement of the correct health and safety models/ framework systems are essential due to the various stakeholders that would be involved in the successful delivery and safety of the event. This would also mean that the wider engagement and frequent liaison with all those who have a vested interest would be essential on a regular basis so that essential timelines so that health and safety actions are implemented in a timely fashion as well as security issues bearing in mind the type of event and potentially the venues and footfall of people passing through various areas. This would most certainly apply in running events where these have been used as a vehicle to increase sport tourism and raising the profile of a destination moving into offering a new service or product. But as well as this music festivals/ carnivals that are passing through a variety, or using a number of venues

The implications for the hallmark event from a health and safety perspective are not too very dissimilar to that of a mega event like the Olympic Games or a Music festival like Glastonbury.

Figure 5. Mouth of the Tyne Festival

Health and Safety in Mega Events.

Mega events and the health and safety need at least 3 to 4 years in planning and because they are over a long duration from those events that have already been highlighted within this chapter.

What has already been established that all events to this end need some sort of robust plan to take into consideration any type of eventuality for those who are working their or those attending? However, due to the nature of Mega events and their duration and attendance a greater thought and detail needs to go into this as there will be contingencies and evacuation plans depending on what issues may occur. There been a number of examples historically where there have been terror attacks, hostages taken and people badly injured or died due to poor planning in these areas therefore there is a greater emphasis on these than ever before. Each situation needs to now form part of the health, safety and risk management plan for a mega event and also must be written into the risk assessment (this will be discussed in later chapters).

Though all eventualities need to be considered and the initial view and perspective of what a mega event is. It would be useful to define what it is? Many academic have put forward their views and perspectives such as Bladen et al (2012):

The term mega events refers to those events that take place for a global media audience and /or that have a significant, long term impacts on economies and societies.

Roche (2000) puts forward his view as;

Mega event as 'large scale cultural (including commercial and sporting) events, which have a dramatic character, mass popular appeal and international significance.

Hall (1997) another academic within the area of events offers a more detailed definition:

Mega events such as World Fairs and Expositions, the World Soccer Cup Final or Olympic Games, are events which are expressly targeted at the international tourism market and may be suitably described as 'mega' by virtue of their size in terms of attendance, target market, level of public financial involvement, political effects, extent of television coverage, construction of facilities, and impact on economic and social fabric of the host community.

What can be clearly noted from those definitions that have been put forward they all share that they are events having a global reach and put a host country/ city into the view through various platforms around the world. They also last a great number of days and therefore their Health and Safety systems/ frameworks need to be even more robust and will be reviewed by the events safety advisory group pre and during the event on a daily basis so that any timely changes can be made immediately and actioned. Kim et al (2019) conceptual model would be the ideal one for this type as the key focuses upon the initial stages on policy are the key factors within this working? Then are the communication processes robust enough ensuring the end product; safety performance is working? Kim et al's (2019) serves as a good model for staging mega events and factors that are listed in Table 1 will form part of this review process daily for health and safety to be effective and efficient for the size, duration and magnitude of an event of this scope.

With this type of an event a greater number of the areas that will need to be covered subcontracted out to suppliers as well as working cohesively with the emergency services as well as the military in some cases. The various Olympics such as London 2012 and Rio 2016 had the armed services dealing security in conjunction with the Law enforcement agencies. Glastonbury Music Festival which becomes a small town after they erect and construct has a highly detailed health and safety policy including everyone's job description, who is responsible for what and also the roles of the emergency services (see appendix 2).

There are noticeable differences between the policies for Glastonbury and The London 2012 Olympics (see appendix 3) that the Olympics is more strategic on how things should be done as such whereas Glastonbury's is as has been mentioned about the roles etc. What would potentially serve as good examples is the two combined as they would then would be fairly comprehensive in their detail.

Each of the types of events that have been detailed have varied in their size and also procedures with regards to health and safety. The last of events that it is worth discussing are those that would be classified as corporate/ business ones.

Health and Safety in Business Events.

Some questions may be raised about what are business events and what is their purpose? By establishing these fundamental questions would enable a better understanding on what areas of health and safety would need to be covered.

Business events are generally commercially motivated which include Meetings, Incentives, Conferences and Exhibitions (MICE). Van Der Wagen and White (2018) highlight that there is a great deal of international competition for business event dollar as the average daily expenditure of business visitors exceeds that of other tourists as Table 2 demonstrates.

Table 2. Business events and attendances. (Adapted Van der Wagen & White, 2018)

Business event	City	Attendees
International Surgery Week	Adelaide	2000
World Lottery Association Convention &Trade Show	Brisbane	800
XXIXth International Horticultural Congress	Brisbane	2000
International Plant Lipid Symposium	Cairns	250
Parliament of the World Religions 2009	Melbourne	10000
Australasian College of Dermatologists	Darwin	700
World Congress of the World Institute of Pain	Perth	2000
105th Rotary International Convention	Sydney	22000

Some countries support the delivery of business events as part of their strategies for various reasons such as investment and trade etc. These are useful reasons as the events tend to be held in one building or conferencing centre and the key areas within health and safety is transport to and from host venues, hotels or any external visits that are undertaken. Each of the venues will have their own health and safety policies which an evet organiser will need to adopt and adapt it to their procedures and systems. Also a key consideration for a health and safety system when external visits which will need to focus on areas injury and death, security and terrorism depending on the type of delegates which links to hostages situations. So the implications of running a business/ corporate can be vary in their nature as they may also contain expos where sellers who provide services for the industry may wish to provide detail on their latest products and services. They tends to be in the same building, especially if it is a conference centre therefore health and safety will need to be detailed in logistical movement and also those setting up, any materials/ substances they may use, sanitation and also the breaking down of their stands.

CLOSING REMARKS

What can be seen that no matter what the size or scale of an event that health and safety plays an imperative role in the delivery of events? The magnitude and detail of what is required, if whether it is for an event that will last a few hours to those that will last a number of days like a mega event will naturally require a greater number of areas to be covered and the number of stakeholders to be involved in the planning process.

What can be seen from the areas that have been discussed and highlighted that a system or framework will need to form part of the planning process which will ensure that all the elements can be covered and also how they will be monitored. Also they would provide attention to detail on the scope of frequency. What be clearly evident that the much bigger events such as a mega event that this will be monitored during the events delivery on a daily basis where as one such as a Hallmark event or Major event it would be as the event is being delivered and then an evaluation would be done at the end of the event.

REFERENCES

Ackapovi, A., & Dizmaikumah, L. (2016). An investigation of health and safety measures in a hydroelectric power plant. *Safety and Health at Work*, *76*(4), 331–339. doi:10.1016/j.shaw.2016.04.006 PMID:27924237

Bistaraki, A., McKeown, E., & Kyratsis, Y. (2019). Legacy interagency planning and collaboration in mass gatherings: Public health and safety in the 20112 London Olympics. *Public Health*, *166*, 19–24. doi:10.1016/j.puhe.2018.09.031 PMID:30439552

Bladen, C., Kennell, J., Abson, E., & Wilde, N. (2012). *Event health, Safety and risk management. In Events Management, an Introduction*. Routledge. doi:10.4324/9780203852972

Bowdin, G., Allen, J., O'Toole, W., Harris, R., & McDonnell, I. (2008). What are events? In Events Management (2nd ed.). Elsevier.

Bowdin, G., Allen, J. O'Toole, W., Harris, R., & McDonnell, I. (2011). Risk Management. In Events Management (3rd ed.). Butterworth-Heinemann.

Change, J. L., & Liang, C. L. (2009). Performance evaluation of process safety management systems of paint manufacturing facilities. *Journal of Loss Prevention in the Process Industries*, *22*(4), 348–402.

Cieslak, T. J. II. (2009). Match day security at Australian sport stadia; a case study of eight venues. *Event Management, 13*(1), 43–54. doi:10.3727/152599509789130566

Couto da Silva, S. L., & Amaral, F. G. (2019). Critical factors of success and barriers to the implementation of occupational health and safety management systems: A systematic review of literature. *Safety Science, 117*, 123–132. doi:10.1016/j.ssci.2019.03.026

Delorenzo, R. A. (1997). Mass gathering medicine; a review. *Prehopsital Disaster Medical., 12*(1), 68–72. doi:10.1017/S1049023X00037250 PMID:10166378

Ferdinand, N., & Kitchin, P. J. (2017). *Risk Management. In Events Management: An International Approach* (2nd ed.). Sage.

Flabouris, A., Nocera, A., & Garner, A. (2004). Efficacy of critical incident monitoring for evaluatying disaster medical readiness and response during the Sydney 2000 Olympic Games. *Prehospital and Disaster Medicine, 19*(2), 164–168. doi:10.1017/S1049023X00001680 PMID:15506253

Getz, D. (2005). *Event Management and Event Tourism* (2nd ed.). New York: Cognizant Communications Corporation.

Getz, D. (2012). *Planning and management of events. In Event Studies; Theory, Research and Policy of Planned Events* (2nd ed.). Routledge.

Getz, D., & Page, S. J. (2016). *Framework for understanding and creat8ing knowledge; planning and management of events. In Event Studies, Theory, research, policy for planned events* (3rd ed.). Routledge.

Hall, C. M. (1997). *Hallmark Tourist Events: Impacts, Management and Planning*. London: Belhaven Press.

Hall, C. M., Timothy, D. J., & Duval, D. T. (2003). *Safety and Security in Tourism; Relationships, Management and Marketing*. New York: Haworth Press.

Health and Safety Executive. (2015). Venue and Site Design. *Event Safety*. www.hse.gov.uk/event-safety

Janiskee, R. (1996). Historic houses and special events. *Annals of Leisure Research, 23*(2), 398–414.

Kim, N., Abdul, K., Rahim, N. F., Iranmanesh, M., & Foroughi, B. (2019). The role of the safety climate in the successful implementation of safety management systems. *Safety Science, 118*, 48–56. doi:10.1016/j.ssci.2019.05.008

Kim, N. S., & Chalip, L. (2004). Why Travel to the FIFA World Cup" Effects of Motives, back ground, interest and constraints. *Tourism Management, 25*(6), 695–707. doi:10.1016/j.tourman.2003.08.011

Meehan, P., Toomey, K. E., Drinnon, J., Cunningham, S., Anderson, N., & Baker, E. (1998). Public Health Response for the 1996 Olympic Games. *American Journal of Medicine Association., 279*(18), 1469–1473. doi:10.1001/jama.279.18.1469 PMID:9600482

Rajaprasd, S. V. S., & Chalapthi, P. V. (2015). Factors influencing implementation of OHHSAS 18001 in Indian construction organisations: Interpretive structural modelling approach. *Safety and Health at Work, 6*(3), 200–205. doi:10.1016/j.shaw.2015.04.001 PMID:26929828

Robson, L. S., Clarke, J. A., Cullen, K., Bielecky, A., Severin, C., Bigelow, P. L., ... Mahood, Q. (2007). The effectiveness of occupational health and safety management system interventions: A systematic review. *Safe. Sci, 45*, 329–353.

Roche, M. (2000). *Mega-Events and Modernity: Olympics and Expos in the Growth of Global Culture*. London: Routledge.

Rutherford-Silvas, J. (2013). *Health and Safety. In Risk Management for Meeting and Events*. Routledge.

Slapper, G. (2007). Corporate Manslaughter Law is a Vast Improvement. *The Times*. www.business.timesonline.co.uk

Sonmez, S. F., & Graefe, A. R. (1998). Influence of terrorism risk on foreign tourism decisions. *Annals of Tourism Research, 25*(1), 112–114. doi:10.1016/S0160-7383(97)00072-8

Taylor, T., & Toohey, K. (2006). Impacts of terrorism-related safety and security measures at a major sport event. *Event Management, 9*(4), 199–209. doi:10.3727/152599506776771544

The Telegraph. (2009). *Hillsborough Timeline; It is 20 years since 96 Liverpool Fans lost their lives at Hillsborough.* www.telegraph.co.uk

The Telegraph. (2012). *The Queens Diamond Jubilee: How to organise a street party.* www.telegraph.co.uk

Van der Wagen, L., & White, L. (2018). *Event Management for tourism, cultural, business and sporting events* (4th ed.). Pearson.

Related Readings

To continue IGI Global's long-standing tradition of advancing innovation through emerging research, please find below a compiled list of recommended IGI Global book chapters and journal articles in the areas of risk assessment, sustainable development, and quality management. These related readings will provide additional information and guidance to further enrich your knowledge and assist you with your own research.

Aital, P., & Vijai, P. (2016). 'Green' Supply Chain Management: Resource Allocation Strategies for Sustainable Operations. In R. Dubey & A. Gunasekaran (Eds.), *Strategic Management of Sustainable Manufacturing Operations* (pp. 1–23). Hershey, PA: IGI Global. doi:10.4018/978-1-5225-0350-7.ch001

Auvray, T., Dallery, T., & Rigot, S. (2017). The Need for News Forms of Financial Intermediation. In L. Saglietto & C. Cezanne (Eds.), *Global Intermediation and Logistics Service Providers* (pp. 143–161). Hershey, PA: IGI Global. doi:10.4018/978-1-5225-2133-4.ch008

Bag, S. (2016). Identifying Green Supply Chain Management Enablers in South African Mining Industry using Ecological Modernization Theory Approach. In R. Dubey & A. Gunasekaran (Eds.), *Strategic Management of Sustainable Manufacturing Operations* (pp. 95–119). Hershey, PA: IGI Global. doi:10.4018/978-1-5225-0350-7.ch005

Bag, S. (2016). Modeling the Soft Skills of Green Procurement Professionals using Interpretive Structural Modeling Approach. In R. Dubey & A. Gunasekaran (Eds.), *Strategic Management of Sustainable Manufacturing Operations* (pp. 120–131). Hershey, PA: IGI Global. doi:10.4018/978-1-5225-0350-7.ch006

Bag, S., Anand, N., & Pandey, K. K. (2017). Green Supply Chain Management Model for Sustainable Manufacturing Practices. In M. Khan, M. Hussain, & M. Ajmal (Eds.), *Green Supply Chain Management for Sustainable Business Practice* (pp. 153–189). Hershey, PA: IGI Global. doi:10.4018/978-1-5225-0635-5.ch006

Balasubramanian, S., & Sundarakani, B. (2017). Assessing the Green Supply Chain Management for the United Arab Emirates Construction Industry. In M. Khan, M. Hussain, & M. Ajmal (Eds.), *Green Supply Chain Management for Sustainable Business Practice* (pp. 83–110). Hershey, PA: IGI Global. doi:10.4018/978-1-5225-0635-5.ch004

Barlatier, P., Giannopoulou, E., & Pénin, J. (2017). Exploring the Role of Open Innovation Intermediaries: The Case of Public Research Valorization. In L. Saglietto & C. Cezanne (Eds.), *Global Intermediation and Logistics Service Providers* (pp. 87–103). Hershey, PA: IGI Global. doi:10.4018/978-1-5225-2133-4.ch005

Bazan, E., & Jaber, M. Y. (2017). The Development and Analysis of Environmentally Responsible Supply Chain Models. In M. Khan, M. Hussain, & M. Ajmal (Eds.), *Green Supply Chain Management for Sustainable Business Practice* (pp. 52–82). Hershey, PA: IGI Global. doi:10.4018/978-1-5225-0635-5.ch003

Bernardes, S., Leite, P., Pesenti, G. S., Viana, E. A., Ladeira, V., Castro, C., ... Renato de Sousa, P. (2017). Information Management Applied to the Development of the Management Process and Improving Energy Efficiency in Transport. In G. Jamil, A. Soares, & C. Pessoa (Eds.), *Handbook of Research on Information Management for Effective Logistics and Supply Chains* (pp. 166–179). Hershey, PA: IGI Global. doi:10.4018/978-1-5225-0973-8.ch009

Bharti, A., & Mittal, A. (2018). Perishable Goods Supply Cold Chain Management in India. In A. Kumar & S. Saurav (Eds.), *Supply Chain Management Strategies and Risk Assessment in Retail Environments* (pp. 232–246). Hershey, PA: IGI Global. doi:10.4018/978-1-5225-3056-5.ch013

Boyonas, M. I., Olavarria, L., & Saenz, M. J. (2016). Scenario Planning: Preparing the Future of Global Supply Chains. In S. Joshi & R. Joshi (Eds.), *Designing and Implementing Global Supply Chain Management* (pp. 51–91). Hershey, PA: IGI Global. doi:10.4018/978-1-4666-9720-1.ch004

Brown, J. R., Bushuev, M. A., Kretinin, A. A., & Guiffrida, A. L. (2017). Recent Developments in Green Supply Chain Management: Sourcing and Logistics. In M. Khan, M. Hussain, & M. Ajmal (Eds.), *Green Supply Chain Management for Sustainable Business Practice* (pp. 191–217). Hershey, PA: IGI Global. doi:10.4018/978-1-5225-0635-5.ch007

Bruno, G. (2017). Identification of Potential Clients, Providers, and Competitors in Supply Chain Networks. In G. Jamil, A. Soares, & C. Pessoa (Eds.), *Handbook of Research on Information Management for Effective Logistics and Supply Chains* (pp. 89–106). Hershey, PA: IGI Global. doi:10.4018/978-1-5225-0973-8.ch005

Cassière, F., & Noireaux, V. (2017). International Distribution: A Cross-Cultural Reading of Intermediation. In L. Saglietto & C. Cezanne (Eds.), *Global Intermediation and Logistics Service Providers* (pp. 243–264). Hershey, PA: IGI Global. doi:10.4018/978-1-5225-2133-4.ch013

Chen, Y. (2018). An Interactive Platform for Sustainable Supply Chains. *International Journal of Interactive Communication Systems and Technologies, 8*(2), 56–73. doi:10.4018/IJICST.2018070104

Costa, E., Soares, A. L., Pinho de Sousa, J., & Jamil, G. L. (2017). Information Management for Network Transformation in Industrial Enterprises Associations: The Case of the Internationalization Process. In G. Jamil, A. Soares, & C. Pessoa (Eds.), *Handbook of Research on Information Management for Effective Logistics and Supply Chains* (pp. 415–436). Hershey, PA: IGI Global. doi:10.4018/978-1-5225-0973-8.ch022

Das, R. (2018). Developing Sustainable Retail Food Value Chain for India: A Challenge for the Next Century. In A. Kumar & S. Saurav (Eds.), *Supply Chain Management Strategies and Risk Assessment in Retail Environments* (pp. 285–300). Hershey, PA: IGI Global. doi:10.4018/978-1-5225-3056-5.ch016

Das, R. (2018). Technologies Enabling Omni-Channel: Understanding Key Success Factors for IT Framework. In A. Kumar & S. Saurav (Eds.), *Supply Chain Management Strategies and Risk Assessment in Retail Environments* (pp. 78–96). Hershey, PA: IGI Global. doi:10.4018/978-1-5225-3056-5.ch005

Edwards, J. S. (2016). Systems for Knowledge Management along the Supply Chain. In S. Joshi & R. Joshi (Eds.), *Designing and Implementing Global Supply Chain Management* (pp. 92–104). Hershey, PA: IGI Global. doi:10.4018/978-1-4666-9720-1.ch005

El Meladi, Y., Glavee-Geo, R., & Buvik, A. (2017). Textile and Clothing Exporting Firms' Evaluation of LSPs' Capabilities and Logistics Outsourcing Performance. In L. Saglietto & C. Cezanne (Eds.), *Global Intermediation and Logistics Service Providers* (pp. 185–207). Hershey, PA: IGI Global. doi:10.4018/978-1-5225-2133-4.ch010

Fattam, N., & Paché, G. (2017). 4PL Intermediation: Exploring Dimensions of Social Capital. In L. Saglietto & C. Cezanne (Eds.), *Global Intermediation and Logistics Service Providers* (pp. 64–85). Hershey, PA: IGI Global. doi:10.4018/978-1-5225-2133-4.ch004

Fernandes da Anunciação, P., Garcia, B., & Fonseca, G. (2017). Importance of Stakeholders Identification in Information Distribution Chain Management for Public Value Detection in Public Initiatives. In G. Jamil, A. Soares, & C. Pessoa (Eds.), *Handbook of Research on Information Management for Effective Logistics and Supply Chains* (pp. 131–146). Hershey, PA: IGI Global. doi:10.4018/978-1-5225-0973-8.ch007

Fernandes da Anunciação, P., Lobo, M., Pereira, O., & Mateus, G. (2017). The Importance of Perception and Appreciation of the Information Management for Effective Logistics and Supply Chain in Transport Sector. In G. Jamil, A. Soares, & C. Pessoa (Eds.), *Handbook of Research on Information Management for Effective Logistics and Supply Chains* (pp. 453–468). Hershey, PA: IGI Global. doi:10.4018/978-1-5225-0973-8.ch024

Fernandes da Anunciação, P., Zambon, A. C., Andrade, F. D., & Sanches de Sousa, C. S. (2017). Competitive Intelligence Competitive Intelligence: A Proposal for Value Creation through Information and Knowledge – The Limeira Gross Domestic Product Sector: Brazil. In G. Jamil, A. Soares, & C. Pessoa (Eds.), *Handbook of Research on Information Management for Effective Logistics and Supply Chains* (pp. 273–286). Hershey, PA: IGI Global. doi:10.4018/978-1-5225-0973-8.ch015

Folinas, D. (2019). Containers in Ports can be Tracked Smartly: Lessons Learned From a Case Study. *International Journal of Applied Logistics*, *9*(1), 39–52. doi:10.4018/IJAL.2019010103

Fonseca, G. L., Rodello, I. A., & Fernandes da Anunciação, P. (2017). Information Management and Enterprise Resource Planning: An Analysis of the Medical Products Distribution Chain. In G. Jamil, A. Soares, & C. Pessoa (Eds.), *Handbook of Research on Information Management for Effective Logistics and Supply Chains* (pp. 334–349). Hershey, PA: IGI Global. doi:10.4018/978-1-5225-0973-8.ch019

Ganguly, A., Chatterjee, D., & Rao, H. V. (2017). Evaluating the Risks Associated with Supply Chain Agility of an Enterprise. *International Journal of Business Analytics*, *4*(3), 15–34. doi:10.4018/IJBAN.2017070102

Ganguly, A., Chatterjee, D., & Talukdar, A. (2019). Knowledge Sharing Barriers Affecting Pharmaceutical Supply Chain Performance. In H. Nozari & A. Szmelter (Eds.), *Global Supply Chains in the Pharmaceutical Industry* (pp. 269–291). Hershey, PA: IGI Global. doi:10.4018/978-1-5225-5921-4.ch012

Giridhar, V., Joshi, R., & Sadarangani, P. H. (2016). Purchase Intentions of Consumer towards Foreign Brand Apparel: Evidences from India. In S. Joshi & R. Joshi (Eds.), *Designing and Implementing Global Supply Chain Management* (pp. 185–209). Hershey, PA: IGI Global. doi:10.4018/978-1-4666-9720-1.ch010

Girisaballa, S., & Bhattacharya, S. (2016). Sustainable Supply Chain: An Institutional Perspective. In R. Dubey & A. Gunasekaran (Eds.), *Strategic Management of Sustainable Manufacturing Operations* (pp. 272–302). Hershey, PA: IGI Global. doi:10.4018/978-1-5225-0350-7.ch012

Golpîra, H. (2017). Supply Chain Network Design Optimization with Risk-Averse Retailer. *International Journal of Information Systems and Supply Chain Management*, *10*(1), 16–28. doi:10.4018/IJISSCM.2017010102

Gunasundari, E. (2019). Best Practices in the Pharmaceutical Supply Chain Management. In H. Nozari & A. Szmelter (Eds.), *Global Supply Chains in the Pharmaceutical Industry* (pp. 228–247). Hershey, PA: IGI Global. doi:10.4018/978-1-5225-5921-4.ch010

Gurtu, A., Searcy, C., & Jaber, M. Y. (2017). Sustainable Supply Chains. In M. Khan, M. Hussain, & M. Ajmal (Eds.), *Green Supply Chain Management for Sustainable Business Practice* (pp. 1–26). Hershey, PA: IGI Global. doi:10.4018/978-1-5225-0635-5.ch001

Herrera, J. E., Argüello, L. V., Gonzalez-Feliu, J., & Jaimes, W. A. (2017). Decision Support System Design Requirements, Information Management, and Urban Logistics Efficiency: Case Study of Bogotá, Colombia. In G. Jamil, A. Soares, & C. Pessoa (Eds.), *Handbook of Research on Information Management for Effective Logistics and Supply Chains* (pp. 223–238). Hershey, PA: IGI Global. doi:10.4018/978-1-5225-0973-8.ch012

Hietajärvi, A., & Karvonen, I. (2016). Management of Risks in Export Networks: The Role of Collaboration. *International Journal of Applied Logistics*, *6*(1), 47–63. doi:10.4018/IJAL.2016010104

Hingley, M., & Vilalta-Perdomo, E. L. (2017). Roles of Intermediaries in Developing Resilient Systems: A Community Approach to Food Micro-Producers. In L. Saglietto & C. Cezanne (Eds.), *Global Intermediation and Logistics Service Providers* (pp. 43–63). Hershey, PA: IGI Global. doi:10.4018/978-1-5225-2133-4.ch003

Hu, J., & Haddud, A. (2017). Exploring the Impact of Globalization and Technology on Supply Chain Management: A Case of International E-Commerce Business. *International Journal of Operations Research and Information Systems, 8*(4), 1–22. doi:10.4018/IJORIS.2017100101

Iltchev, P., Palczewska, A., Pilichowska, K., Kozlowski, R., & Marczak, M. (2017). Benefits of the Transics Fleet Management System. In G. Jamil, A. Soares, & C. Pessoa (Eds.), *Handbook of Research on Information Management for Effective Logistics and Supply Chains* (pp. 287–302). Hershey, PA: IGI Global. doi:10.4018/978-1-5225-0973-8.ch016

Jamil, G. L. (2017). Numbers Can Restrict Results?: Qualitative Research Methods as Information and Knowledge Management Support in Supply Chain and Logistics Sectors. In G. Jamil, A. Soares, & C. Pessoa (Eds.), *Handbook of Research on Information Management for Effective Logistics and Supply Chains* (pp. 1–22). Hershey, PA: IGI Global. doi:10.4018/978-1-5225-0973-8.ch001

Jamil, G. L., & Jamil, C. C. (2017). Information and Knowledge Management Perspective Contributions for Fashion Studies: Observing Logistics and Supply Chain Management Processes. In G. Jamil, A. Soares, & C. Pessoa (Eds.), *Handbook of Research on Information Management for Effective Logistics and Supply Chains* (pp. 199–221). Hershey, PA: IGI Global. doi:10.4018/978-1-5225-0973-8.ch011

Janawade, V. (2017). Perceived Quality of an Intermediary and Its Relations with Image and Perceived Value: An Insight from the Case of Airline Alliances. In L. Saglietto & C. Cezanne (Eds.), *Global Intermediation and Logistics Service Providers* (pp. 286–316). Hershey, PA: IGI Global. doi:10.4018/978-1-5225-2133-4.ch015

Jeble, S. C. (2016). Sustainable Supply Chain Management: Literature Review. In R. Dubey & A. Gunasekaran (Eds.), *Strategic Management of Sustainable Manufacturing Operations* (pp. 303–330). Hershey, PA: IGI Global. doi:10.4018/978-1-5225-0350-7.ch013

Joshi, B. P., & Kumar, S. (2016). Intuitionistic Fuzzy Sets-Based Method for Multi-Criteria Decision-Making. In S. Joshi & R. Joshi (Eds.), *Designing and Implementing Global Supply Chain Management* (pp. 22–35). Hershey, PA: IGI Global. doi:10.4018/978-1-4666-9720-1.ch002

Joshi, R., & Joshi, S. (2016). Assessing the Readiness of Farmers towards Cold Chain Management: Evidences from India. In S. Joshi & R. Joshi (Eds.), *Designing and Implementing Global Supply Chain Management* (pp. 219–235). Hershey, PA: IGI Global. doi:10.4018/978-1-4666-9720-1.ch012

Jridi, K., Jaziri-Bouagina, D., & Triki, A. (2017). The SCM, CRM Information System, and KM – An Integrating Theoretical View: The Case of Sales Force Automation. In G. Jamil, A. Soares, & C. Pessoa (Eds.), *Handbook of Research on Information Management for Effective Logistics and Supply Chains* (pp. 239–254). Hershey, PA: IGI Global. doi:10.4018/978-1-5225-0973-8.ch013

Kaiwartya, O., Tiwari, P. K., Kumar, S., & Prasad, M. (2016). Dynamic Vehicle Routing Solution in the Framework of Nature-Inspired Algorithms. In S. Joshi & R. Joshi (Eds.), *Designing and Implementing Global Supply Chain Management* (pp. 36–50). Hershey, PA: IGI Global. doi:10.4018/978-1-4666-9720-1.ch003

Kasemsap, K. (2016). The Role of Sustainable Performance Measurement System in Global Supply Chain. In R. Dubey & A. Gunasekaran (Eds.), *Strategic Management of Sustainable Manufacturing Operations* (pp. 331–348). Hershey, PA: IGI Global. doi:10.4018/978-1-5225-0350-7.ch014

Kasemsap, K. (2016). The Roles of Lean and Green Supply Chain Management Strategies in the Global Business Environments. In S. Joshi & R. Joshi (Eds.), *Designing and Implementing Global Supply Chain Management* (pp. 152–173). Hershey, PA: IGI Global. doi:10.4018/978-1-4666-9720-1.ch008

Kasemsap, K. (2017). Advocating Information System, Information Integration, and Information Sharing in Global Supply Chain. In G. Jamil, A. Soares, & C. Pessoa (Eds.), *Handbook of Research on Information Management for Effective Logistics and Supply Chains* (pp. 107–130). Hershey, PA: IGI Global. doi:10.4018/978-1-5225-0973-8.ch006

Kasemsap, K. (2017). Advocating Sustainable Supply Chain Management and Sustainability in Global Supply Chain. In M. Khan, M. Hussain, & M. Ajmal (Eds.), *Green Supply Chain Management for Sustainable Business Practice* (pp. 234–271). Hershey, PA: IGI Global. doi:10.4018/978-1-5225-0635-5.ch009

Kasemsap, K. (2017). The Roles of Logistics Service Providers and Supply Chain Integration in Global Supply Chain. In L. Saglietto & C. Cezanne (Eds.), *Global Intermediation and Logistics Service Providers* (pp. 265–285). Hershey, PA: IGI Global. doi:10.4018/978-1-5225-2133-4.ch014

Kasemsap, K. (2018). Enhancing Closed-Loop Supply Chain in Global Supply Chain. In A. Kumar & S. Saurav (Eds.), *Supply Chain Management Strategies and Risk Assessment in Retail Environments* (pp. 159–180). Hershey, PA: IGI Global. doi:10.4018/978-1-5225-3056-5.ch009

Kasemsap, K. (2018). Retail Management and Electronic Retailing. In A. Kumar & S. Saurav (Eds.), *Supply Chain Management Strategies and Risk Assessment in Retail Environments* (pp. 139–158). Hershey, PA: IGI Global. doi:10.4018/978-1-5225-3056-5.ch008

Kozlowski, R., Iltchev, P., Palczewska, A., Pilichowska, K., & Marczak, M. (2017). Analysis of the Possibility to Implement the Transics System and GBOX Assist Systems in a Selected Company. In G. Jamil, A. Soares, & C. Pessoa (Eds.), *Handbook of Research on Information Management for Effective Logistics and Supply Chains* (pp. 303–315). Hershey, PA: IGI Global. doi:10.4018/978-1-5225-0973-8.ch017

Kros, J. F., Liao, Y., Kirchoff, J. F., & Zemanek, J. E. Jr. (2019). Traceability in the Supply Chain. *International Journal of Applied Logistics*, *9*(1), 1–22. doi:10.4018/IJAL.2019010101

Kwon, I. G., Hong, S., & Kim, S. (2017). Do Collaborative Relationships in Supply Chain Pay-Off? *International Journal of Organizational and Collective Intelligence*, *7*(1), 36–46. doi:10.4018/IJOCI.2017010103

Lahmar, A., Chabchoub, H., Galasso, F., & Lamothe, J. (2018). The VESP Model: A Conceptual Model of Supply Chain Vulnerability. *International Journal of Risk and Contingency Management*, *7*(2), 42–66. doi:10.4018/IJRCM.2018040103

Lahmar, A., Galasso, F., Lamothe, J., & Chabchoub, H. (2018). Classification Essay of SCRM Research. In A. Kumar & S. Saurav (Eds.), *Supply Chain Management Strategies and Risk Assessment in Retail Environments* (pp. 213–230). Hershey, PA: IGI Global. doi:10.4018/978-1-5225-3056-5.ch012

Lambourdière, E., Verny, J., & Corbin, E. (2017). Exploring the Sources of the Competitive Advantage of Logistics Service Providers. In L. Saglietto & C. Cezanne (Eds.), *Global Intermediation and Logistics Service Providers* (pp. 163–184). Hershey, PA: IGI Global. doi:10.4018/978-1-5225-2133-4.ch009

Lazzareschi, V. H., & Brito, M. S. (2017). Strategic Information Management: Proposal of Business Project Model. In G. Jamil, A. Soares, & C. Pessoa (Eds.), *Handbook of Research on Information Management for Effective Logistics and Supply Chains* (pp. 59–88). Hershey, PA: IGI Global. doi:10.4018/978-1-5225-0973-8.ch004

Leu, J., Lee, L. J., & Krischke, A. (2016). Value Engineering-Based Method for Implementing the ISO14001 System in the Green Supply Chains. *International Journal of Strategic Decision Sciences*, *7*(4), 1–20. doi:10.4018/IJSDS.2016100101

Lima de Magalhães, J., & Moreira, A. (2017). Information Systems Management in the Supply Chain in an Official Pharmaceutical Laboratory. In G. Jamil, A. Soares, & C. Pessoa (Eds.), *Handbook of Research on Information Management for Effective Logistics and Supply Chains* (pp. 350–373). Hershey, PA: IGI Global. doi:10.4018/978-1-5225-0973-8.ch020

Liotard, I., & Revest, V. (2017). Intermediation and Innovation Contests on the Internet: Lessons from the Study of Two Platforms. In L. Saglietto & C. Cezanne (Eds.), *Global Intermediation and Logistics Service Providers* (pp. 104–122). Hershey, PA: IGI Global. doi:10.4018/978-1-5225-2133-4.ch006

Lopes, B., Falcão, L., & Canellas, T. (2017). Supply-Side: Mapping High Capacity Suppliers of Goods and Services. In G. Jamil, A. Soares, & C. Pessoa (Eds.), *Handbook of Research on Information Management for Effective Logistics and Supply Chains* (pp. 147–165). Hershey, PA: IGI Global. doi:10.4018/978-1-5225-0973-8.ch008

Loya, V. M., Alcaraz, J. L., Reza, J. R., & Gayosso, D. G. (2017). The Impact of ICT on Supply Chain Agility and Human Performance. In G. Jamil, A. Soares, & C. Pessoa (Eds.), *Handbook of Research on Information Management for Effective Logistics and Supply Chains* (pp. 180–198). Hershey, PA: IGI Global. doi:10.4018/978-1-5225-0973-8.ch010

Mani, V., Agrawal, R., Sharma, V., & Kavitha, T. N. (2016). Supply Chain Social Sustainability and Manufacturing. In R. Dubey & A. Gunasekaran (Eds.), *Strategic Management of Sustainable Manufacturing Operations* (pp. 149–175). Hershey, PA: IGI Global. doi:10.4018/978-1-5225-0350-7.ch008

Messina, D., Santos, C., Soares, A. L., & Barros, A. C. (2017). Risk and Visibility in Supply Chains: An Information Management Perspective. In G. Jamil, A. Soares, & C. Pessoa (Eds.), *Handbook of Research on Information Management for Effective Logistics and Supply Chains* (pp. 34–57). Hershey, PA: IGI Global. doi:10.4018/978-1-5225-0973-8.ch003

Mohammadi, M., & Mukhtar, M. (2017). A Service-oriented Methodology for Supporting Business Process Architecture Layers in Supply Chain Management. *International Journal of Information Systems and Supply Chain Management, 10*(4), 18–43. doi:10.4018/IJISSCM.2017100102

Moradeyo, A. A. (2018). Understanding Supply Chain Collaboration and Risk Management. *International Journal of Risk and Contingency Management, 7*(3), 42–52. doi:10.4018/IJRCM.2018070102

Mostafa, S., & Dumrak, J. (2017). A Waste Elimination Process: An Approach for Lean and Sustainable Manufacturing Systems. In M. Khan, M. Hussain, & M. Ajmal (Eds.), *Green Supply Chain Management for Sustainable Business Practice* (pp. 111–152). Hershey, PA: IGI Global. doi:10.4018/978-1-5225-0635-5.ch005

Mukherjee, S., & Mukerjee, A. (2016). Sustainable Business Development by Responding to Climate Change: A Case of the Tata Group. In R. Dubey & A. Gunasekaran (Eds.), *Strategic Management of Sustainable Manufacturing Operations* (pp. 176–191). Hershey, PA: IGI Global. doi:10.4018/978-1-5225-0350-7.ch009

Nageswar, A. K., & Yellampalli, S. (2019). Distributed Trust Using Blockchain for Efficient Pharmaceutical Supply Chain. In H. Nozari & A. Szmelter (Eds.), *Global Supply Chains in the Pharmaceutical Industry* (pp. 248–268). Hershey, PA: IGI Global. doi:10.4018/978-1-5225-5921-4.ch011

Najar, T., & Amami, M. (2019). Supply Chain and Inter-Organizational Information Systems Role. In H. Nozari & A. Szmelter (Eds.), *Global Supply Chains in the Pharmaceutical Industry* (pp. 27–55). Hershey, PA: IGI Global. doi:10.4018/978-1-5225-5921-4.ch002

Negi, S., & Anand, N. (2018). Wastage and Cold Chain Infrastructure Relationship in Indian Food Supply Chain: A Study From Farm to Retail. In A. Kumar & S. Saurav (Eds.), *Supply Chain Management Strategies and Risk Assessment in Retail Environments* (pp. 247–266). Hershey, PA: IGI Global. doi:10.4018/978-1-5225-3056-5.ch014

Nikabadi, M. S., & Hajihoseinali, A. (2018). E-Waste Recycling System in Closed Loop Supply Chain. *International Journal of System Dynamics Applications*, *7*(2), 55–80. doi:10.4018/IJSDA.2018040104

Ogonowska, M. (2017). Convention and Visitors Bureau: A Key Intermediary in the Events Industry. In L. Saglietto & C. Cezanne (Eds.), *Global Intermediation and Logistics Service Providers* (pp. 226–241). Hershey, PA: IGI Global. doi:10.4018/978-1-5225-2133-4.ch012

Osiecka-Brzeska, K. (2019). Sustainable Supply Chain as a Part of CSR Strategy: The Example of Polpharma, Poland. In H. Nozari & A. Szmelter (Eds.), *Global Supply Chains in the Pharmaceutical Industry* (pp. 293–315). Hershey, PA: IGI Global. doi:10.4018/978-1-5225-5921-4.ch013

Özdemir, E., & Yılmaz, M. (2018). Omni-Channel Retailing: The Risks, Challenges, and Opportunities. In A. Kumar & S. Saurav (Eds.), *Supply Chain Management Strategies and Risk Assessment in Retail Environments* (pp. 97–118). Hershey, PA: IGI Global. doi:10.4018/978-1-5225-3056-5.ch006

Pal, K. (2018). Building High Quality Big Data-Based Applications in Supply Chains. In A. Kumar & S. Saurav (Eds.), *Supply Chain Management Strategies and Risk Assessment in Retail Environments* (pp. 1–24). Hershey, PA: IGI Global. doi:10.4018/978-1-5225-3056-5.ch001

Panwar, N., Uniyal, D., & Rautela, K. S. (2016). Mapping Sustainable Tourism into Emergency Management Structure to Enhance Humanitarian Networks and Disaster Risk Reduction using Public-Private Partnerships (PPP) Initiatives in Himalayan States: The Global Supply Chain Issues and Strategies. In S. Joshi & R. Joshi (Eds.), *Designing and Implementing Global Supply Chain Management* (pp. 129–151). Hershey, PA: IGI Global. doi:10.4018/978-1-4666-9720-1.ch007

Pessoa, C. R., & Júnior, M. D. (2017). A Telecommunications Approach in Systems for Effective Logistics and Supply Chains. In G. Jamil, A. Soares, & C. Pessoa (Eds.), *Handbook of Research on Information Management for Effective Logistics and Supply Chains* (pp. 437–452). Hershey, PA: IGI Global. doi:10.4018/978-1-5225-0973-8.ch023

Pessoa, C. R., & Marques, M. E. (2017). Information Technology and Communication Management in Supply Chain Management. In G. Jamil, A. Soares, & C. Pessoa (Eds.), *Handbook of Research on Information Management for Effective Logistics and Supply Chains* (pp. 23–33). Hershey, PA: IGI Global. doi:10.4018/978-1-5225-0973-8.ch002

Petrisor, I., & Cozmiuc, D. (2017). Global Supply Chain Management Organization at Siemens in the Advent of Industry 4.0. In L. Saglietto & C. Cezanne (Eds.), *Global Intermediation and Logistics Service Providers* (pp. 123–142). Hershey, PA: IGI Global. doi:10.4018/978-1-5225-2133-4.ch007

Poças Rascão, J. (2017). Information System for Logistics and Distribution Management. In G. Jamil, A. Soares, & C. Pessoa (Eds.), *Handbook of Research on Information Management for Effective Logistics and Supply Chains* (pp. 374–414). Hershey, PA: IGI Global. doi:10.4018/978-1-5225-0973-8.ch021

Polat, O. (2017). An Overview of Feeder Services in the Era of Mega Containerships. In L. Saglietto & C. Cezanne (Eds.), *Global Intermediation and Logistics Service Providers* (pp. 317–339). Hershey, PA: IGI Global. doi:10.4018/978-1-5225-2133-4.ch016

Ponnusamy, S. K., & Christopher, F. C. (2019). Production Process in the Pharmaceutical Industry. In H. Nozari & A. Szmelter (Eds.), *Global Supply Chains in the Pharmaceutical Industry* (pp. 158–179). Hershey, PA: IGI Global. doi:10.4018/978-1-5225-5921-4.ch007

Ponnusamy, S. K., & Ragini, Y. P. (2019). Product Lifecycle in the Pharmaceutical Industry. In H. Nozari & A. Szmelter (Eds.), *Global Supply Chains in the Pharmaceutical Industry* (pp. 112–132). Hershey, PA: IGI Global. doi:10.4018/978-1-5225-5921-4.ch005

Ponnusamy, S. K., & Saravanan, A. (2019). Characteristics of Pharmaceutical Supply Chains. In H. Nozari & A. Szmelter (Eds.), *Global Supply Chains in the Pharmaceutical Industry* (pp. 181–205). Hershey, PA: IGI Global. doi:10.4018/978-1-5225-5921-4.ch008

Quillaud, A. (2017). A Framework for Thinking Intermediation in Logistics Management. In L. Saglietto & C. Cezanne (Eds.), *Global Intermediation and Logistics Service Providers* (pp. 19–42). Hershey, PA: IGI Global. doi:10.4018/978-1-5225-2133-4.ch002

Ragini, Y. P. (2019). Pharmaceutical Development Process. In H. Nozari & A. Szmelter (Eds.), *Global Supply Chains in the Pharmaceutical Industry* (pp. 133–157). Hershey, PA: IGI Global. doi:10.4018/978-1-5225-5921-4.ch006

Rana, P., & Pandey, D. (2016). Challenges and Issues in E-Banking Services and Operations in Developing Countries. In S. Joshi & R. Joshi (Eds.), *Designing and Implementing Global Supply Chain Management* (pp. 237–281). Hershey, PA: IGI Global. doi:10.4018/978-1-4666-9720-1.ch013

Saglietto, L. (2017). Intermediary and Intermediation: Which Logistics Services? In L. Saglietto & C. Cezanne (Eds.), *Global Intermediation and Logistics Service Providers* (pp. 1–18). Hershey, PA: IGI Global. doi:10.4018/978-1-5225-2133-4.ch001

Saha, S. K., & Jha, A. (2018). Role of Information Technology on Supply Chain Management of Pharmaceutical Industry. *International Journal of Applied Logistics*, *8*(2), 39–68. doi:10.4018/IJAL.2018070103

Saravanan, A. (2019). Pharmaceutical and Life Sciences Supply Chain Management. In H. Nozari & A. Szmelter (Eds.), *Global Supply Chains in the Pharmaceutical Industry* (pp. 206–227). Hershey, PA: IGI Global. doi:10.4018/978-1-5225-5921-4.ch009

Saththasivam, G., & Fernando, Y. (2017). Integrated Sustainable Supply Chain Management: Current Practices and Future Direction. In M. Khan, M. Hussain, & M. Ajmal (Eds.), *Green Supply Chain Management for Sustainable Business Practice* (pp. 218–233). Hershey, PA: IGI Global. doi:10.4018/978-1-5225-0635-5.ch008

Satolo, E. G., Simon, A. T., & Braga, S. S. Jr. (2016). Sustainable Development and the Integration of Normative Standards. In R. Dubey & A. Gunasekaran (Eds.), *Strategic Management of Sustainable Manufacturing Operations* (pp. 192–226). Hershey, PA: IGI Global. doi:10.4018/978-1-5225-0350-7.ch010

Saurav, S. (2018). Realizing the Potential of Retail Analytics. In A. Kumar & S. Saurav (Eds.), *Supply Chain Management Strategies and Risk Assessment in Retail Environments* (pp. 60–76). Hershey, PA: IGI Global. doi:10.4018/978-1-5225-3056-5.ch004

Saurav, S. (2018). Supply Chain Management in Pharmaceutical Industry: Opportunities and Challenges for Retailers. In A. Kumar & S. Saurav (Eds.), *Supply Chain Management Strategies and Risk Assessment in Retail Environments* (pp. 267–284). Hershey, PA: IGI Global. doi:10.4018/978-1-5225-3056-5.ch015

Shafiu, I., Wang, W. Y., & Singh, H. (2016). Information Security Compliance Behaviour of Supply Chain Stakeholders: Influences and Differences. *International Journal of Information Systems and Supply Chain Management, 9*(1), 1–16. doi:10.4018/IJISSCM.2016010101

Sharma, M., & Kumar, J. (2016). Operational Efficacy of 3PL in Reverse Logistics and Closed Loop Supply Chain: Service Quality Challenges in Emerging Markets. In S. Joshi & R. Joshi (Eds.), *Designing and Implementing Global Supply Chain Management* (pp. 106–128). Hershey, PA: IGI Global. doi:10.4018/978-1-4666-9720-1.ch006

Shibin, K. T. (2016). Enablers of Sustainable Manufacturing Overview, Framework and Further Research Directions. In R. Dubey & A. Gunasekaran (Eds.), *Strategic Management of Sustainable Manufacturing Operations* (pp. 52–73). Hershey, PA: IGI Global. doi:10.4018/978-1-5225-0350-7.ch003

Simão, J. C., & Fernandes da Anunciação, P. (2017). Port Single Window and Logistics Single Window: Two Competitiveness Proposals in the Port Value Chain. In G. Jamil, A. Soares, & C. Pessoa (Eds.), *Handbook of Research on Information Management for Effective Logistics and Supply Chains* (pp. 316–333). Hershey, PA: IGI Global. doi:10.4018/978-1-5225-0973-8.ch018

Singh, A., Panackal, N., & Venkataramani, B. (2016). Environmental Accounting for Industrial Growth and Sustainable Development in India: An Overview and Theoretical Framework. In R. Dubey & A. Gunasekaran (Eds.), *Strategic Management of Sustainable Manufacturing Operations* (pp. 74–94). Hershey, PA: IGI Global. doi:10.4018/978-1-5225-0350-7.ch004

Singh, H. (2018). Applications of Intelligent Video Analytics in the Field of Retail Management: A Study. In A. Kumar & S. Saurav (Eds.), *Supply Chain Management Strategies and Risk Assessment in Retail Environments* (pp. 42–59). Hershey, PA: IGI Global. doi:10.4018/978-1-5225-3056-5.ch003

Singh, N. K. (2018). Designing Distribution Centres for Omni-Channel Fulfilment: In Indian Context. In A. Kumar & S. Saurav (Eds.), *Supply Chain Management Strategies and Risk Assessment in Retail Environments* (pp. 119–137). Hershey, PA: IGI Global. doi:10.4018/978-1-5225-3056-5.ch007

Singh, R., & Sankhi, A. (2016). An Empirical Study on Factors Leading to Employee Retention for Manufacturing Industry in India. In R. Dubey & A. Gunasekaran (Eds.), *Strategic Management of Sustainable Manufacturing Operations* (pp. 24–51). Hershey, PA: IGI Global. doi:10.4018/978-1-5225-0350-7.ch002

Singh, S., Olugu, E. U., & Musa, S. N. (2016). Development of Key Performance Measures for Sustainable Manufacturing in Global SMEs. In S. Joshi & R. Joshi (Eds.), *Designing and Implementing Global Supply Chain Management* (pp. 210–218). Hershey, PA: IGI Global. doi:10.4018/978-1-4666-9720-1.ch011

Smriti, K. (2018). Building an Effective Customer Loyalty Program. In A. Kumar & S. Saurav (Eds.), *Supply Chain Management Strategies and Risk Assessment in Retail Environments* (pp. 195–212). Hershey, PA: IGI Global. doi:10.4018/978-1-5225-3056-5.ch011

Smriti, K. (2018). Predicting Online Returns. In A. Kumar & S. Saurav (Eds.), *Supply Chain Management Strategies and Risk Assessment in Retail Environments* (pp. 181–194). Hershey, PA: IGI Global. doi:10.4018/978-1-5225-3056-5.ch010

Soares, E. R., & Zaidan, F. H. (2017). Composition of the Financial Logistic Costs of the IT Organizations Linked to the Financial Market: Financial Indicators of the Software Development Project. In G. Jamil, A. Soares, & C. Pessoa (Eds.), *Handbook of Research on Information Management for Effective Logistics and Supply Chains* (pp. 255–272). Hershey, PA: IGI Global. doi:10.4018/978-1-5225-0973-8.ch014

Sousa, M. J., Cruz, R., Dias, I., & Caracol, C. (2017). Information Management Systems in the Supply Chain. In G. Jamil, A. Soares, & C. Pessoa (Eds.), *Handbook of Research on Information Management for Effective Logistics and Supply Chains* (pp. 469–485). Hershey, PA: IGI Global. doi:10.4018/978-1-5225-0973-8.ch025

Srivastav, G., & Rawat, P. S. (2016). Indian Handicraft and Globalization: The Export Context. In S. Joshi & R. Joshi (Eds.), *Designing and Implementing Global Supply Chain Management* (pp. 175–184). Hershey, PA: IGI Global. doi:10.4018/978-1-4666-9720-1.ch009

Strang, K. D., & Vajjhala, N. R. (2017). Student Resistance to a Mandatory Learning Management System in Online Supply Chain Courses. *Journal of Organizational and End User Computing, 29*(3), 49–67. doi:10.4018/JOEUC.2017070103

Subramanian, K., Joshi, K. P., & Deshmukh, S. (2018). Improving Forecasting for Customer Service Supply Chain Using Big Data Analytics. In A. Kumar & S. Saurav (Eds.), *Supply Chain Management Strategies and Risk Assessment in Retail Environments* (pp. 25–41). Hershey, PA: IGI Global. doi:10.4018/978-1-5225-3056-5.ch002

Suganya, S. (2019). Global Macrotrends in Pharmaceutical Industry. In H. Nozari & A. Szmelter (Eds.), *Global Supply Chains in the Pharmaceutical Industry* (pp. 86–110). Hershey, PA: IGI Global. doi:10.4018/978-1-5225-5921-4.ch004

Szmelter, A. (2019). Global Pharmaceutical Industry: Characteristics and Trends. In H. Nozari & A. Szmelter (Eds.), *Global Supply Chains in the Pharmaceutical Industry* (pp. 57–85). Hershey, PA: IGI Global. doi:10.4018/978-1-5225-5921-4.ch003

Szmelter, A. (2019). Logistics Thinking: The Basics of Logistics. In H. Nozari & A. Szmelter (Eds.), *Global Supply Chains in the Pharmaceutical Industry* (pp. 1–26). Hershey, PA: IGI Global. doi:10.4018/978-1-5225-5921-4.ch001

Tambo, T., & Mikkelsen, O. E. (2016). Fashion Supply Chain Optimization: Linking Make-to-Order Purchasing and B2B E-Commerce. In S. Joshi & R. Joshi (Eds.), *Designing and Implementing Global Supply Chain Management* (pp. 1–21). Hershey, PA: IGI Global. doi:10.4018/978-1-4666-9720-1.ch001

Tiwari, A., Kumar, K., & Roy, S. (2016). Sustainable Non Traditional Manufacturing Processes: A Case with Electrochemical Machining (ECM). In R. Dubey & A. Gunasekaran (Eds.), *Strategic Management of Sustainable Manufacturing Operations* (pp. 227–271). Hershey, PA: IGI Global. doi:10.4018/978-1-5225-0350-7.ch011

Vanany, I., & Syamil, A. (2016). Teaching Supply Chain Management Using an Innovative Practical Game. *International Journal of Information Systems and Supply Chain Management, 9*(4), 82–99. doi:10.4018/IJISSCM.2016100105

Vargas-Hernández, J. G., & Hernández, A. I. (2019). Collaboration in the Mexican Pharmaceutical Industry: An Analysis Within the Institutional Framework. In H. Nozari & A. Szmelter (Eds.), *Global Supply Chains in the Pharmaceutical Industry* (pp. 316–333). Hershey, PA: IGI Global. doi:10.4018/978-1-5225-5921-4.ch014

Venkatesh, V., & Luthra, S. (2016). Role of Sustainable Procurement in Sustainable Manufacturing Operations: An Indian Insight. In R. Dubey & A. Gunasekaran (Eds.), *Strategic Management of Sustainable Manufacturing Operations* (pp. 132–148). Hershey, PA: IGI Global. doi:10.4018/978-1-5225-0350-7.ch007

Vijayan, G., & Kamarulzaman, N. H. (2017). An Introduction to Sustainable Supply Chain Management and Business Implications. In M. Khan, M. Hussain, & M. Ajmal (Eds.), *Green Supply Chain Management for Sustainable Business Practice* (pp. 27–50). Hershey, PA: IGI Global. doi:10.4018/978-1-5225-0635-5.ch002

Vlachos, I. P., & Gutnik, S. (2016). Together We E-Export: Horizontal Cooperation Among Austrian Food Companies in Global Supply Chains and the Role of Electronic Business Tools. *International Journal of Information Systems and Supply Chain Management, 9*(1), 17–40. doi:10.4018/IJISSCM.2016010102

Yavuz, M., & Deligönül, B. (2017). The Importance of Logistics Information Technologies and Knowledge Management Capabilities on Intermediaries' Performance. In L. Saglietto & C. Cezanne (Eds.), *Global Intermediation and Logistics Service Providers* (pp. 208–225). Hershey, PA: IGI Global. doi:10.4018/978-1-5225-2133-4.ch011

About the Contributors

Vipin Nadda is working as Lecturer and Programme Manager (Postgraduate-Tourism & Hospitality) with University of Sunderland in London. Some of his previous responsibilities involved Lecturer in tourism and hospitality management at Oxford House College, London and Kurukshetra University in India. He also freelance as 'consultant' for Confederation of tourism and Hospitality, Anglia Ruskin University, BPP University and Cardiff Metropolitan University. He has more than twenty years of experience in education, Industry and research and besides PhD in tourism, also written book Chapters, published four books, attended, presented papers in various international conferences/seminars and organised International academic conferences. He is Editor-in Chief for International Journal of Entrepreneurship Management Development and Innovation. As an experienced academician, he has been Lecturing/teaching a variety of subjects ranging from, Strategic tourism development, Destination branding, global tourism, sustainable tourism development, hospitality management studies, Tourism Marketing and International Hospitality Marketing, Marketing strategy, International business environment, Applied Research Methods, supervising MBA, MSc, and PhD Dissertation projects in UK as well as overseas. Dr. Nadda has been also actively involved in development of Programme at different awarding bodies. He has been working with confederation of tourism and hospitality awarding body based at London as an exam board member, external examiner and assessor for last seven years and has helped to develop level-5/6 qualifications for them, which are Ofqual, recognised and delivered globally. He has international exposure, having taught students from various nationalities, which evidences his adaptability, diversity and multi-levelled skills.

Ian Arnott has written published academic papers in the field of sports events management and is also a practitioner in event management delivery. Therefore, his knowledge is both that of an academic, disseminating this to future event managers who are studying as well those who work in the industry today. Part of the process when he is working in the delivery is working with key stakeholders in the emergency services and also National Governing Bodies in sport.

As well as this, Ian feels for those who wish to embark on a career in the industry, it's important that they get a wealth of experiences, so they can understand the diversity of the industry. Therefore, he works with key providers at local, national and international level to expose the future events managers and practitioners the opportunities to work alongside them gaining invaluable knowledge and experience.

Wendy Sealy is a destination and tourism product-marketing expert helping tourism businesses to increase their revenue yield. She is a motivational speaker and as an entrepreneur is the owner of Crystal Jewells. Dr. Sealy has been lecturing since 2005. Before joining the University of Chichester, she taught at the undergraduate and post-graduate level in Tourism Management at Buckinghamshire New University and at the postgraduate level in Sport and Event Management at the University of the West-Indies. Dr. Sealy graduated from the University of the West Indies with a first class honours degree in History and Sociology. She later completed her masters degree in Tourism Marketing with distinction at the University of Surrey and her Doctor of Philosophy degree with Brunel University, London. Dr. Sealy is responsible for coordinating the teaching, learning and research activities for the BA (Hons) Event Management within the Business School.She is responsible for employer-student engagement activity and the co-ordination of live event projects under the provision of the event management degree programme. Wendy is particularly interested in the experiences of event management students in higher education and has spent a considerable amount of time conducting research and publishing work in this area. She is the creator of the Event Management Body of Skills (EMBOS) model for event management education, published in Event Management – an International Journal. Her other interest involves experimenting with different ways to embed employability into the students' higher education experiences in order to ensure that they can compete for jobs at graduation. She is also the Associate Editor of the Journal of Tourism and Sustainability and a member of the editorial committee of the Journal of International Tourism and Hospitality.Dr. Sealy has published her research in several academic journals and books including the Journal of Travel and Tourism Marketing, the Journal of Travel Research and The International Journal on Tourism and Sustainability.

* * *

Dhanwant Dadwal is currently a freelance education consultant with Dadwal consultants London. She has MSc in Information Technology and MA in sociology. Dhanwant has wide experience in operations, administration, health & safety, and strategic marketing & sales in the travel and tourism industry.

Sumesh S. Dadwal is an academician and a consultant based in London, UK. Currently, he is a faculty member, Program Leader, Internship Lead and Dissertation research Lead for Masters Programs at London Campus of Northumbria University (working in partnership with QAHE) London, UK. He has 20 years of experience in business academic research, teaching, e-learning, quality assurances and in a wide range of business, technology-enabled business models, tourism and Healthcare subjects. He is actively engaged in postgraduate and Ph.D. research supervision. Dr. Dadwal's core areas of expertise Include International Marketing & Globalisation, Contemporary and Technological trends in the marketing & consumer behaviour, strategic & technological innovation management. He is an active researcher undertaking analysis in the service sector, promotional strategies in the emerging markets, Digital Marketing, Augmented Reality Marketing and consumer behaviour, utilising various qualitative and quantitative techniques. He has written various research papers, co-edited a book, written book chapters, and has lead research activities at various levels. He has successfully undertaken projects that required data mining, editing and undertaken quantitative research methods using software Excel, SPSS. Dr. Dadwal has also had been associated with the Quality Assurance Agency (QAA) of UK., as a Reviewer for Educational quality Oversight at UK higher educational Institution. He has also worked as a freelance consultant with a number of institutions and an awarding organisation (OTHM, UK) for the development of new educational programmes. Besides this, Sumesh is also a freelance consultant (business analysis) for emerging markets and also Member of Advisory and Editorial Boards of Academics at some journals of repute. Dr. Dadwal has taught at a number of London campuses of the UK Universities such as University of London (Birkbeck College), University of Glyndwr, Roehampton University, Plymouth University, Ulster University, University of West London, New Bucks University, Northampton University, and Northumbria University UK.

Maximiliano E. Korstanje is editor in chief of International Journal of Safety and Security in Tourism (UP Argentina) and International Journal of Cyber Warfare and Terrorism (IGI-GlobalUS). Besides being Senior Researchers in the Department of Economics at University of Palermo, Argentina, he is a global affiliate of Tourism Crisis Management Institute (University of Florida US), Centre for Ethnicity and Racism Studies (University of Leeds), Now he co-edits almost 10 specialized journals in such themes as human rights, mobility, tourism and terrorism. Korstanje is subject to biographical records for Marquis Who`s Who in the World since 2009. He had nominated to 5 honorary doctorates for his contribution in the study of the effects of terrorism in tourism. In 2015 he was awarded as Visiting Research Fellow at School of Sociology and Social Policy, University of Leeds, UK.

Emma Nolan has 25 years' experience as an event management practitioner and an academic. This includes working in visitor attractions, theatres and local authorities and delivering events for a variety of clients including political parties, the TUC and the NHS. Emma moved into academic in 2008 and worked as a Senior Lecturer in Project and Event Management at the University of Winchester for several years. Emma is a Senior Fellow of the HEA, has an MA in Education and is currently working towards her PhD at the University of Chichester. Emma recently published her first book, Working with Venues for Events (Routledge, 2018), and her current research interests are centered on the MICE sector. She is specifically interested in exploring the site selection process in the organisation of association conferences.

Bilan Sahidi is a senior lecturer and Programme Manager at University of Sunderland in London. He is holder of a PhD in Philosophy, Politics and Sociology from the RWTH-Aachen University (Germany). He holds also three masters' in Business (University of Sunderland), Marketing & Innovation from Anglia Ruskin University and Strategy. He is specialised in the Hegelian Philosophy and very active in the current research on the Ultimate foundation of Raison and ethics.

Index

Ensure Quality Research is Introduced to the Academic Community

Become an IGI Global Reviewer for Authored Book Projects

The overall success of an authored book project is dependent on quality and timely reviews.

In this competitive age of scholarly publishing, constructive and timely feedback significantly expedites the turnaround time of manuscripts from submission to acceptance, allowing the publication and discovery of forward-thinking research at a much more expeditious rate. Several IGI Global authored book projects are currently seeking highly-qualified experts in the field to fill vacancies on their respective editorial review boards:

Applications and Inquiries may be sent to:
development@igi-global.com

Applicants must have a doctorate (or an equivalent degree) as well as publishing and reviewing experience. Reviewers are asked to complete the open-ended evaluation questions with as much detail as possible in a timely, collegial, and constructive manner. All reviewers' tenures run for one-year terms on the editorial review boards and are expected to complete at least three reviews per term. Upon successful completion of this term, reviewers can be considered for an additional term.

If you have a colleague that may be interested in this opportunity, we encourage you to share this information with them.

www.ingramcontent.com/pod-product-compliance
Lightning Source LLC
LaVergne TN
LVHW081330021026
849161LV00008BA/1832
9781799832300